Modernist Studies
Rima Drell Reck, Editor

AMERICAN EXPATRIATE WRITING
AND THE PARIS MOMENT

AMERICAN EXPATRIATE WRITING AND THE PARIS MOMENT

MODERNISM AND PLACE

Donald Pizer

Louisiana State University Press
Baton Rouge and London

Copyright © 1996 by Louisiana State University Press
All rights reserved
Manufactured in the United States of America
First printing
05 04 03 02 01 00 99 98 97 96   5 4 3 2 1

Designer: Michele Myatt
Display typeface: Parisian
Text typeface: Bembo
Typesetter: Impressions, Inc.
Printer and binder: Thomson-Shore, Inc.

LIBRARY OF CONGRESS CATALOGING-IN-PUBLICATION DATA

Pizer, Donald.
    American expatriate writing and the Paris moment : modernism and
place / Donald Pizer.
        p.   cm. — (Modernist studies)
    Includes bibliographical references (p.   ) and index.
    ISBN 0-8071-2026-X (alk. paper)
    1. American literature—France—Paris—History and criticism.
    2. American literature—20th century—History and criticism.
    3. Paris (France)—Intellectual life—20th century.   4. Americans—
    France—Paris—History—20th century.   5. American literature—
    French influences.   6. Modernism (Literature)—France—Paris.
    7. Modernism (Literature)—United States.   8. Paris (France)—In
    literature.   I. Title.   II. Series.
    PS159.F5P59   1996
    810.9'813044361—dc20   95-38307
                                                                   CIP

Portions of this book appeared previously in different form as "The Sexual Geography of Expatriate Paris," in *Twentieth Century Literature,* XXXVI (1990), 173–85, and as "American Expatriate Autobiography and the Paris Moment," in *South Carolina Review,* XXVII (1995), 250–57.

Now, I participated in an actual marriage of material with immaterial things; I celebrated an immediate reconciling of spirit and flesh, forever and now, heaven and earth. Paris was for me precisely and complexly this homogeneous duality: this accepting transcendence; this living and dying more than death or life. Whereas . . . New York had reduced mankind to a tribe of pygmies, Paris (in every shape and gesture and avenue and cranny of her being) was continuously expressing the humanness of humanity. Everywhere I sensed a miraculous presence, not of mere children and women and men, but of living human beings; and the fact that I could scarcely understand their language seemed irrelevant, since the truth of our momentarily mutual aliveness created an imperishable communion. While . . . a once rising and striving world toppled into withering hideously smithereens, love rose in my heart like a sun and beauty blossomed in my life like a star. Now, finally and first, I was myself: a temporal citizen of eternity; one with all human being born and unborn.

    —E. E. Cummings, *i—six nonlectures*

New skies the exiles find, but the heart remains the same.

    —Horace, *Epistles*

CONTENTS

ILLUSTRATIONS

PREFACE

The American expatriate movement has received much attention almost from its origin, and books of every kind dealing with it, from
memoirs and anecdotal histories to tour guides and coffee-table photograph collections, continue to appear regularly.[1] The movement, however, has attracted surprisingly limited attention as a body of literary
expression with its own significant themes and shapes.[2] Much has been
written, often retelling the same tired anecdotes, about the personal
relationships within the America expatriate community in Paris between the wars, but little has appeared that concentrates on the fiction
and autobiography that derives from and depicts this significant moment
in American cultural and literary history. The focus of *American Expatriate Writing and the Paris Moment: Modernism and Place* is therefore on
the texts themselves as they participate in the creation of a mythic
expression of American self-exile in Paris during the 1920s and 1930s.
I wish to explore the works that I discuss not for their reference to

1. In addition to the memoirs cited in the Selected Bibliography, by such figures as Sylvia
Beach, Morley Callaghan, Caresse Crosby, John Dos Passos, Harold Loeb, and Harold Stearns,
representative examples of these genres include, among anecdotal histories, Noël Riley Fitch's
Sylvia Beach and the Lost Generation: A History of Literary Paris in the Twenties and Thirties (New
York, 1983) and Humphrey Carpenter's *Geniuses Together: American Writers in Paris in the 1920s*
(London, 1987); among tour guides, Brian N. Morton's *Americans in Paris* (New York, 1986) and
Arlen J. Hansen's *Expatriate Paris: A Cultural and Literary Guide to Paris of the 1920s* (New York,
1990); and among photograph collections, Robert J. Gajdusek's *Hemingway's Paris* (New York,
1978) and William Wiser's *The Crazy Years: Paris in the Twenties* (New York, 1983).
2. Although three valuable and important critical studies have appeared within the last decade,
each of these discusses expatriate writing in a way that differs significantly from my approach.
Shari Benstock's *Women of the Left Bank: Paris, 1900–1940* (Austin, Tex., 1986) is limited to
women writers, is largely biographical, and includes British as well as American figures. Jean
Méral's *Paris in American Literature* (Chapel Hill, N.C., 1989) surveys the entire history of American
writing about Paris, with only brief comments about specific works of the 1920s and 1930s. J.
Gerald Kennedy's *Imagining Paris: Exile, Writing, and American Identity* (New Haven, 1993), which
appeared when my study was almost completed, approaches expatriate writing between the wars
largely in relation to issues of cultural identity.

actual events and people—though this kind of inquiry does occur when critically relevant—but rather for their expression of a cluster of felt responses to Paris and the expatriate experience. The study thus seeks to answer two interrelated questions: What are the common threads in the evocation of expatriate Paris among these works, common threads that in the aggregate constitute a coherent response to the Paris moment by the expatriate generation? And, How does each work achieve its own distinctive expression of the common experience of expatriation?

These inquiries are important for several reasons. Exile is, of course, a common phenomenon of twentieth-century history. But, more narrowly, self-exile by American artists and intellectuals between the wars is a dramatic example of a major characteristic of early-twentieth-century American life: the alienation of the artist from the norms of his culture. In addition, almost all the most significant works of expatriate fiction and autobiography are experimental in technique and form. Two of the central characteristics of the rich vein that is American high modernism between the wars—the deeply critical response of the American writer to his society and his attempt to express this response in new ways—are therefore represented suggestively and powerfully by expatriate writing. The various strands of cubistic spatial form, dramatic representation of consciousness, and sexual explicitness which I trace in the work of the major expatriate writers of the 1920s and 1930s reach a climactic synthesis in Henry Miller's *Tropic of Cancer,* in which the writer as artist in rebellion exists within a radically re-created mythic Paris. Thus, by realizing more clearly the relationship of a major expatriate work by Ernest Hemingway, Gertrude Stein, Anaïs Nin, John Dos Passos, F. Scott Fitzgerald, or Henry Miller to the Paris moment— how the evocation of Paris in the work participates in a general response and also constitutes a unique thematic and formal element in the particular work—we gain a greater understanding of the mythic moment in general, of the role of the moment in the expression of a modernist aesthetic, and of the distinctive nature of the specific work.

It is because I wish most of all to explore the neglected question of how the depiction of the Paris scene helps shape and control the themes and forms of specific works that I have decided to discuss individual works at length and to limit myself to major works. I have no doubt omitted expatriate writing that other critics with other aims would find significant and deserving of inclusion—Djuna Barnes's *Nightwood,* for example, or Robert McAlmon and Kate Boyle's *Being Geniuses Together, 1920–1930,* or Malcolm Cowley's *Exile's Return: A Narrative of Ideas.*

Nevertheless, the works selected represent, I believe, both the basic configuration of and best expression within expatriate writing.

Two other aspects of my approach should be noted. After offering a brief introduction to the theme of self-exile in early-twentieth-century American writing, I organize the study by genre, because of the significant thematic difference between the autobiographical and the fictional expression of the expatriate experience in Paris. In addition, though my emphasis is on American writing that derives from the writer's residence in Paris between the wars, I include some works that either are set earlier (the opening portion of Stein's *Autobiography of Alice B. Toklas*) or were written or revised later (Hemingway's memoir and Nin's diaries). This is only an apparent anomaly, however, both because it is principally genre rather than chronology that creates difference in expatriate expression, and because the myth of the Paris moment for this generation has an almost synchronic unity.

I am indebted to Richard M. Frazer, Jr., J. Gerald Kennedy, Richard Lehan, and Rima Drell Reck for various kindnesses during the writing of this study, and especially to Carol Pizer for her editorial skill.

AMERICAN EXPATRIATE WRITING
AND THE PARIS MOMENT

PROLOGUE
THE SHAPE OF THE MYTH

Reduced to its most fundamental level, the expatriate or self-exile state of mind is compounded out of the interrelated conditions of the rejection of a homeland and the desire for and acceptance of an alternative place. The world one has been bred in is perceived to suffer from intolerable inadequacies and limitations; another world seems to be free of these failings and to offer a more fruitful way of life. Although it can be contended that this state of mind has existed since the beginning of civilization, the specific characteristics of expatriation—the particular stifling conditions of one's time and place, the particular appeal of a different set of conditions—have varied in nature and degree from historical moment to historical moment. I would therefore like to suggest in this introduction some of the distinguishing characteristics of the widespread tendency during the early twentieth century for American writers to reject American life in favor of life in Paris. And since my interest in this study is not in a sociological or quantitatively historical analysis of American expatriation between the wars—of how many Americans arrived in Paris each year and of where they stayed and what they did—but in the beliefs and values of American expatriate writers as expressed in their own writing about the expatriate experience, in the mythic statement of expatriation, in short, I will introduce the subject by means of several works of fiction that, in relation to one another, suggest the basic character of the interplay between repulsion and attraction for this generation.

Gertrude Stein's "The Good Anna," from *Three Lives* (1909), Ernest Hemingway's "Soldier's Home," from *In Our Time* (1925), and Henry James's account of Lambert Strether's visit to Gloriani's garden, from *The Ambassadors* (1903), are all in their various ways expatriate works even though they do not—unlike the works I will discuss in the main part of this book—deal directly with the expatriate experience. All were written after their authors had become expatriates, and all therefore, whether in the depiction of the limitations of American life or of the appeal of Paris, reflect the almost inevitable impulse in the treatment of these subjects to offer an apologia for the condition of self-exile.

Gertrude Stein sets "The Good Anna" in the German-American world of turn-of-the-century Baltimore—the Bridgepoint of the story. Anna, who spends her life as a housekeeper for middle-class employers, is "good" in the sense that she is thrifty, hardworking, religious, and moralistic. These qualities make life difficult for her—"You see that Anna led an arduous and troubled life"—because her employers and acquaintances lack the qualities and Anna sees it as her duty to put things "to rights."[1] Most of her employers are like Miss Mathilda, for whom Anna works for many years, in enjoying a good time and being careless about money, whereas Anna, whose "face was worn, her cheeks . . . thin, her mouth drawn and firm" (13), labors and worries.

Anna is especially severe in her attitude toward sexual transgressions, as Stein initially renders comically by introducing it in relation to Anna's concern over the "wickedness" of her dogs, which were "under strict orders never to be bad one with the other [since] periods of evil thinking came very regularly" (12–13). A more significant revelation of Anna's nature lies in her response to Miss Mathilda's distinctive form of wickedness: "And then Miss Mathilda loved to go out on joyous, country tramps when, stretching free and far with cheerful comrades, over rolling hills and cornfields, glorious in the setting sun, and dogwood white and shining underneath the moon and clear stars over head, and brilliant air and tingling blood, it was hard to have to think of Anna's anger at the late return" (22). The passage expresses the force of Anna's moralism by contrasting an open and rich natural life with the psychological and emotional restrictions placed on enjoying that life by the presence of a censor. The "good" life, as defined by Anna's beliefs and actions, excludes not only obvious derelictions, such as the

---

1. Gertrude Stein, *Three Lives* (1909; rpr. New York, n.d.), 13, 39. Further citations of this edition will appear in the text.

sexual, but any act of the spirit which is "wasteful" in the sense of being morally unsanctioned or economically unproductive. And since all in the community—even those who resent Anna's admonitions and rebel against them—accept the premise that she is indeed the "good Anna" and that her values constitute a proper and necessary norm for conduct and belief, Anna is, despite her "arduous" and "troubled" life, a figure of power and control in the world where she functions. Hers is the voice of righteousness, and though that voice may breed opposition, those who rebel are, like her dogs, willful and sinful in their rebellion.

Stein in "The Good Anna" thus portrays an America dominated by an ethos in which the principal commitments are to work, money, and self-discipline (especially in sexual matters), with these constituting both godliness and community worthiness. Many of course fail to live up to the expectations of the ethos, but the expectations—the belief that such commitments constitute the "good" life—pass unchallenged. Miss Mathilda, after many years with Anna, finally goes abroad to live, where she can buy "a bit of porcelain, a new etching and sometimes even an oil painting" (21) without fear of being chastised for excess. But Anna remains in America, still the "good" Anna.

Hemingway's "Soldier's Home" recapitulates Stein's dissection of the power of a normative moralism in American life but also relates its rejection to the war. Krebs, before his two years in the marines, is a standard product of middle-class America. From a small Oklahoma town where his father is in real estate, he has gone to a Methodist college in Kansas. A college photograph reveals him "among his fraternity brothers, all of them wearing exactly the same height and style collar."[2]

The war, however, introduces him to the fundamental human realities of death and sex. He fights in several major battles, and after the war he acquires a "not beautiful" (69) German girl friend. Returning home, he has difficulty fitting his life back into the prescribed grooves of belief and behavior. One problem—and this is a theme that Hemingway and Dos Passos were to exploit more fully in *A Farewell to Arms* and *Three Soldiers*—is that he is disgusted by the convention of "exaggeration" and "untruth" (70) that war needs had imposed on accounts of combat and that he is forced to fall in with in the telling of his own

---

2. Ernest Hemingway, *In Our Time* (1925; rpr. New York, 1970), 69. Further citations of this edition will appear in the text.

war experiences. He now begins to extrapolate from his understanding of the convention of the lie in wartime to a recognition of its prevalence in his everyday life. As Ezra Pound had put it a few years earlier in his "Hugh Selwyn Mauberly," those who fought

> walked eye-deep in hell
> believing in old-men's lies, then unbelieving
> came home, home to a lie,
> home to many deceits, home to old lies.

Another problem is that Krebs now realizes, from the perspective of his greater range of experience, that he cannot accept his community's belief that life consists of work, money, and religion. These two barriers to reintegration into his world coalesce in his decision to opt out of both community values and community-sanctioned behavior. He expresses his withdrawal most clearly in his attitude toward the girls of the town, girls he finds desirable but not desirable enough to break out of his isolation. "He did not want to get into the intrigue and the politics. He did not want to have to do any courting. He did not want to tell any more lies. It wasn't worth it" (71).

Withdrawal, however, is not an acceptable strategy within Krebs's world, and his parents seek to prod him into reentry. Other young men his age are working and getting married and "are on their way to being really a credit to the community" (75), his mother tells him. When Krebs balks, his mother brings out the heavy artillery of familial love and religious faith. "Don't you love your mother, dear boy?" and "Would you kneel and pray with me, Harold?" (75–76) are questions she puts to him under the assumption that both she and he accept the premise that a child's love for his mother and his religious belief are intimately related to his role as an American. Krebs responds positively to both questions because he feels sorry for his mother. But he thinks to himself that "he would go to Kansas City" (77) to escape the "consequences" and "complications" that conventional belief is imposing on him at home. Earlier, in relation to his interest in the girls of the town, he had recalled his girl friend in Germany. It had been "simple" there, he remembers. "He did not want to leave Germany. He did not want to come home" (72). Indeed, the stories in *In Our Time* that follow "Soldier's Home" and pursue the experiences of an American protagonist who has served in the war are, with the exception of the final story, "Big Two-Hearted River," set in Europe. The implication is that Krebs will continue the process of self-exile he begins by leaving for Kansas City and will return to Europe, where human relationships are "simpler" in that they lack the "consequences" imposed upon them by an American middle-class value system.

The attractiveness of Europe for a Miss Mathilda or a Krebs as a way out of the coercive moralism of American life—as a place where the spirit might roam freely and where one could be true to one's feelings without regard to being a credit to the community—had already been emphatically localized in Paris by Henry James in *The Ambassadors*. The middle-aged writer Lambert Strether has led a dull and vaguely unsatisfying life in Woollett, Massachusetts, a town not depicted but the tone of which comes across—largely through the references to Strether's patroness Mrs. Newsome, and the comportment of the Woollett Pococks in Paris—as the moral and emotional equivalent of Miss Mathilda's Baltimore and Krebs's Oklahoma backwater. Strether finds himself in Paris on appointment by Mrs. Newsome to rescue her son from the dangers of Parisian idleness and the possibility of a mésalliance and to return him to work and a proper marriage in Woollett.

Not long after his arrival, Strether is taken to a reception given by the artist Gloriani in the garden of one of the "old noble houses" in the Faubourg Saint-Germain.[3] The intellectual and spiritual density and vibrancy that Strether almost immediately senses in the scene appear to derive principally from the other guests' "liberty to be as they were" (124). "His fellow guests were multiplying, and these things, their liberty, their intensity, their variety, their conditions at large, were in fusion in the admirable medium of the scene" (124). Gloriani himself—"a fine worn handsome face, a face that was like an open letter in a foreign tongue" (125)—also evinces this unique receptivity and freedom and richness, and Strether has the "consciousness of opening . . . all the windows of his mind, of letting this rather grey interior drink in for once the sun of a clime not marked in his old geography" (125).

Gloriani, in keeping with his name, embodies a resplendent mix of freedom and energy, a mix uniting the best in art, society, and nature—as is implied by the setting of an artist's reception in the garden of a fine old house—and explicitly in tune with the new "geography" of Paris rather than the old of Woollett. It is no wonder that, having "drunk in" this potion and having realized as well that despite its

3. Henry James, *The Ambassadors* (1903; rpr. New York, 1960), 124. Further citations of this edition will appear in the text.

invigorating effect it has come too late for him, Strether admonishes the much younger American, Little Bilham, to "live all you can; it's a mistake not to. . . . This place and these impressions . . . have had their abundant message for me, have just dropped *that* into my mind" (137). They have also, of course, helped establish the mythic reality of Paris as the "place" where Americans can lead the kind of life represented in Strether's "impressions" of Gloriani's garden party—a place where the open windows of the receptive spirit can absorb the sun and thus where the gray moral and spiritual climate of Woollett can be exchanged for an atmosphere of a radiant richness and freedom.

THE MOMENT
REMEMBERED AND IMAGINED:
AUTOBIOGRAPHY

Ernest Hemingway
A Moveable Feast

The first impression left by Ernest Hemingway's memoir of his Paris apprenticeship is that it consists of a number of loosely connected anecdotal sketches dominated by the author's animus toward his fellow expatriates.[1] With the exception of two sequences of sketches—those on Gertrude Stein and F. Scott Fitzgerald—each sketch is an independent unit with little evident relationship, either in subject matter or causality, to the adjacent sketches. The only immediately evident principle of form for the volume lies in the division of Hemingway's Paris experiences into two vaguely outlined temporal and geographical parts.[2] The first portion of the book, until "Ford Madox Ford and the Devil's Disciple," is loosely situated within the Hemingways' years at the place de la Contrescarpe, from their arrival in Paris in late 1921 to their departure for Canada in the summer of 1923. The second portion,

---

1. The most valuable biographical account of Hemingway's expatriate period is Michael S. Reynolds' *Hemingway: The Paris Years* (Oxford, 1989). Jacqueline Tavernier-Courbin (*Ernest Hemingway: L'Education européenne de Nick Adams* [Paris, 1978]) relates Hemingway's expatriation to major themes in his early fiction.

2. Gerry Brenner ("Are We Going to Hemingway's *Feast?*" *American Literature,* LIV [1982], 528–44) and Jacqueline Tavernier-Courbin (*Ernest Hemingway's "A Moveable Feast": The Making of Myth* [Boston, 1991]) have demonstrated that Mary Hemingway and Scribner's performed various editorial functions in preparing the manuscript of *A Moveable Feast* for posthumous publication, including shifting the order of some sketches and selecting, from several extant versions, the text for the last chapter. Since this editorial work did not insert any material not by Hemingway, and since, as I will argue, Hemingway's conception of his Paris years was more synchronic than diachronic, I will discuss *A Moveable Feast* as complete and integral in its published form.

except for the concluding chapter set in Schruns, often relates to their life in the Montparnasse quartier after their return from Canada in January, 1924, until mid-1926, during the time they occupied a flat above a sawmill on the rue Notre-Dame-des-Champs. The major continuity in the two phases appears to be Hemingway's desire to undercut, through selective reportage, the personal and literary reputations of those figures with whom he had quarreled over the years or whose reputations rivaled his own.

Thus, though *A Moveable Feast* seeks to tell two profound personal stories—how Hemingway matured as an artist in Paris but also how his marriage collapsed—both of these seem obscured and diffused by the miscellaneous shape and the satiric edge of the work. Yet, Hemingway's primary intent in *A Moveable Feast*—to exhibit the growth of an artist's sensibility and capability in a setting ideally suited to that end—is not defeated by the seemingly random shape and bitchy tone of the volume but is rather served by these and other ostensible anomalies in the work's makeup. Hemingway, as the author of an autobiography concentrating on a writer's relationship to a place, makes the specific characteristics of that place metaphoric equivalents of his developing identity as a writer.[3] And to Hemingway, as he sought not long before his death to define this identity, the specifics that appeared most aptly and powerfully to render his sense of emerging selfhood could be found in the seemingly miscellaneously selected and organized recollections of the people, places, and events of the Paris of his younger years. To put the matter another way, *A Moveable Feast* conveys Hemingway's understanding of his Paris moment not by sequential narrative, fully developed characterization, and consistency of tone—the prose equivalents of the representational in painting—but rather (as in his earlier *In Our Time*) by the cubist technique of fragmentation of the whole (the moment which the artist is attempting to depict) into its disparate and discontinuous parts.[4] This modernist technique entails an

---

3. Among critical works that have contributed to my understanding of the nature of literary autobiography are Robert Langbaum's *The Mysteries of Identity: A Theme in Modern Literature* (Chicago, 1977), Leonard Lutwack's *The Role of Place in Literature* (Syracuse, N.Y., 1984), James Olney's *Metaphors of Self: The Meaning of Autobiography* (Princeton, 1972), and Roy Pascal's *Design and Truth in Autobiography* (Cambridge, Mass., 1960).

4. The relationship of Hemingway's work to the visual arts has received considerable attention. See especially Emily S. Watts, *Ernest Hemingway and the Arts* (Urbana, Ill., 1971); Meyly Chin Hagemann, "Hemingway's Secret: Visual to Verbal Art," *Journal of Modern Literature,* VII (1979), 87–112; and Kenneth G. Johnston, "Hemingway and Cézanne: Doing the Country," *American Literature,* LVI (1984), 28–37.

Rue Mouffetard off the place de la Contrescarpe in the early twenties
Roger-Viollet, Paris

intellectualization of experience by the writer through the act of fragmentation and a complementary intellectualization or conceptualization
by the reader if he is to gather a sense of the whole from its parts.

"A Good Café on the Place St.-Michel," the first sketch in *A Moveable
Feast,* introduces the central motifs of the entire work. Hemingway
begins not with his and Hadley's arrival in Paris in December, 1921,
but with their life the following winter, when they are thoroughly
settled in their flat off the place de la Contrescarpe and when he has
begun to develop his own distinctive vision and style as a writer. He
makes clear, in the opening paragraphs of the sketch, that this growth
has not occurred within the context of the expatriate cafés of Montparnasse. The Café des Amateurs, in the place de la Contrescarpe, is a
"sad, evilly run café." Frequented by foul-smelling drunkards, it is the
"cesspool" of the quartier. Hemingway's image reminds him that the
area, lacking sewers, requires a constant emptying of its cesspools, "and
the odor was very strong."[5] The quartier's seedy café, its excremental

5. Ernest Hemingway, *A Moveable Feast* (1964; rpr. New York, 1987), 3–4. Further citations
of this edition will appear in the text.

miasma, and the cold, dank Paris winter refute the popular notion of the writer as a carefree bohemian. This is working-class Paris, in which, it is implied, the writer as worker has been finding his way.

The cheap room in the quartier which Hemingway has been renting as a studio is too cold, however, and so we find him, in the first of his many walks in *A Moveable Feast,* making his way to a "good café" on the place Saint-Michel, a "pleasant café, warm and clean and friendly" (5). (It is striking that Hemingway never in *A Moveable Feast* writes of traveling by Metro, autobus, or taxi. To him, at least in memory, Paris is a city where he reaches his destination on foot.) There he orders a coffee and begins to write a story set in Michigan. He has already, he notes, written several similar stories, "and in one place you could write about it better than in another. That was called transplanting yourself, I thought, and it could be as necessary with people as with other sorts of growing things" (5).

Although Hemingway in this instance uses a specific horticultural image for the act of self-exile by the writer, he is of course referring more generally to mobility and its consequent freedom as a key benefit of expatriation. He has already expressed in miniature, in the opening paragraphs of the sketch, the equation of mobility with creativity. He has been stifled by the inhospitable Contrescarpe quartier and its cafés, and so he frees himself of their reek and cold by walking the mile or so to the "good café" near the Seine, where he can begin to write. Paris, as Henry Miller notes in *Tropic of Cancer,* "of itself initiates no dramas. They are begun elsewhere. Paris is simply an obstetrical instrument that tears the living embryo from the womb and puts it in the incubator. Paris is the cradle of artificial births. Rocking here in the cradle each one slips back into his soil."[6] Movement, in one of the great paradoxes the condition of exile holds for the modern artist, above all stimulates the creative expression of that which was "begun elsewhere"—in this instance, Hemingway's "up in Michigan" youth. And though any act of transplanting might theoretically be beneficial, it is Paris above all, as Miller implies, that has served as the best "obstetrical instrument."

Hemingway's walk past the Pantheon, down the boulevard Saint-Michel, and across the boulevard Saint-Germain to the place Saint-Michel is thus a symbolic reenactment of transplantation in the sense both of expatriation and of the freedom of movement possible within

6. Henry Miller, *Tropic of Cancer* (1934; rpr. New York, 1961), 29.

Paris itself in order to select the ambience best suited to a particular
artistic effort. In his accounts of his movements through the city, many
of them detailed street by street, Hemingway develops a trope of a
world of multiple contexts for the writer and of the writer's freedom
to select the ones he desires. On this occasion, he chooses the "good
café" over the Café des Amateurs, as he will later choose the Closerie
des Lilas over the Rotonde or Sélect. He will choose to walk down
the rue Notre-Dame-des-Champs to box with Pound at Pound's flat
but not to join Pound in the effete and lesbian salon world of Natalie
Barney on the rue Jacob. And he will direct his journey from the place
de la Contrescarpe to Stein's residence, on the rue de Fleurus, through
the Jardin du Luxembourg so he can study the Cézannes at the Musée
du Luxembourg. Paris, in other words, is not like the Good Anna's
Baltimore and Krebs's Oklahoma town with their one-dimensionality,
in which the only choice is to accept or reject the dominant social and
moral code. It is itself an image of freedom in that it harbors—in its
quartiers, its residents, and its activities—a sufficient range of life to
dramatize how freedom of choice, and therefore, as in transplanting, a
fuller growth, lie within one's capacity simply through an act of movement.

Early in *A Moveable Feast,* Hemingway and Hadley decide to take a
walk. He suggests that they should go

"down by the river and along the quais."

"Let's walk down the rue de Seine and look in all the galleries and
in the windows of the shops."

"Sure. We can walk anywhere and we can stop at some new café
where we don't know anyone and nobody knows us and have a drink."
(37)

"We can walk anywhere," Hemingway remarks. It is thus no wonder
that he walks constantly in *A Moveable Feast* and that the trope of
freedom through physical movement also dominates the powerfully
affirmative portrayals of Paris as a city of growth for the artist in Anaïs
Nin's diaries and Miller's *Tropic of Cancer.*

As Hemingway is writing his story in the "good café," a pretty girl
enters.

I looked at her and she disturbed me and made me very excited. I
wished I could put her in the story, or anywhere, but she had placed

herself so she could watch the street and the entry and I knew she was waiting for someone. So I went on writing.

The story was writing itself and I was having a hard time keeping up with it. I ordered another Rum St. James and I watched the girl whenever I looked up, or when I sharpened the pencil with a pencil sharpener. . . .

I've seen you, beauty, and you belong to me now, whoever you are waiting for and if I never see you again, I thought. You belong to me and all Paris belongs to me and I belong to this notebook and this pencil.

Then I went back to writing and I entered far into the story and was lost in it. . . . Then the story was finished and I was very tired. (5–6)

The imagery of the moment is at once beautifully transparent and richly suggestive. Sexual desire for the pretty girl is deflected into the sharpened pencil and becomes a potent force for creative rather than sexual fulfillment. But the union of sexual and creative energy is more complex than this, since the girl's beauty and desirability, and thus the excitement engendered by her, are equated with Paris itself ("You belong to me and all Paris belongs to me"). Hemingway can establish this equation because the girl, in the heightened sexuality she introduces into the café, constitutes as well the intensity and excitement of his responsiveness to the city as a whole. The moment, in brief, fuses sexual potency and the idea of Paris into a dynamic flow of creative expression. The girl and Paris belong to Hemingway—that is, have been absorbed into his consciousness. And "I belong to this notebook and this pencil": that is, the girl and Paris are themselves being transmuted into art in the sense of the power they have unleashed.

Hemingway in this passage broaches one of the major tropes in the depiction of expatriate Paris, not only for himself but for all expatriate writing centering on the city. The image of Paris as the city of light aptly renders the intellectual openness and intensity that earlier generations of Americans abroad had associated with the city. But for expatriates of the twenties and thirties, Paris was above all a world of sexual freedom—a place where the writer could feel desire, could translate (if he or she wished) desire into action, and could write about desire. As will become apparent, the depiction of the nature and consequences of desire differs markedly from writer to writer. But all the expatriate writers found in the reality behind Hemingway's image of the sharpened pencil—in sex free to acknowledge itself—a powerful source of creative freedom and strength.

Hemingway himself, in *A Moveable Feast,* put the trope of creative potency in ruthlessly heterosexual and almost puritan terms. The scene in the "good café" is legitimatized for Hemingway by virtue of involving a male who desires a female and by virtue of the desire's being only felt, not acted out. Other forms of sexuality in Hemingway's Paris world, especially homosexuality, are harshly dealt with. Hemingway depicts homosexuality negatively throughout his work, but in *A Moveable Feast* the depiction is directly related to the trope of creative potency. So, in an obvious extended example, the homosexual Hal (in the sketch "Birth of a New School"), who is suffering from writer's block, "invades" the Closerie des Lilas and interrupts Hemingway's own efforts to write. Angry and resentful, Hemingway suggests to Hal that "if you can't write why don't you learn to write criticism" and thereby "help your own people." After all, he adds, "creation's probably overrated" (95).

Hemingway's bald linking in this sketch of a failure in creative energy and what he believed to be a failure in sexuality is pursued with more point and less crudity in his portraits of Stein and Fitzgerald. He portrays both writers (as I will shortly discuss more fully) as lacking in the strength of will necessary to work hard and honestly at their craft, and in both instances he associates this insufficiency in creative energy with a sexual weakness. Like most visitors to the rue de Fleurus, Hemingway noted that Stein played the masculine role of conversing with the guest while Toklas undertook the feminine one of entertaining the guest's wife. So far so good in Hemingway's sexual structuring of experience, since Stein, as an artist, is the masculine figure in the household, a role confirmed by her peasant appearance and directive manner. But Stein lacks the capacity to work hard at her writing through assiduous revision—a crucial weakness to Hemingway—and this failure in strength is also played out and confirmed in her sexual relationship to Toklas. In Hemingway's final sketch on Stein, "A Strange Enough Ending," he recounts overhearing a conversation between Stein and Toklas in which "Miss Stein's voice came pleading and begging, saying 'Don't, pussy. Don't. Don't, please don't. I'll do anything, pussy, but please don't do it. Please don't. Please don't, pussy' " (118). Hemingway clearly intends, in this climactic account of his relationship with Stein, to offer an explanation of her essential weakness as writer and person. She may have defended lesbianism to Hemingway as less crude and ugly than male homosexuality, but her relationship to Toklas, in which her abject pleading casts her in the feminine role of sexual subjugation, links her with Hal in their common lack of strength, both sexually and creatively.

Something of the same narrative strategy and the same metaphoric relationship between sexual roles and artistic potency occurs in the sketches concerning Fitzgerald, though in the more conventional context of marriage. Fitzgerald is portrayed at the start as a talented writer who has betrayed his integrity to write stories for well-paying popular magazines. But as Hemingway comes to know Fitzgerald more fully, he realizes that it is Zelda who is the key not only to Fitzgerald's earlier prostituting of his talent but also to his later inability to write anything. "Zelda was jealous of Scott's work" (180), Hemingway flatly declares, and she therefore exploited her husband's susceptibility to alcohol to prevent him from working. Here again Hemingway's depiction of a failure in creative potency ends climactically in a scene in which the artist reveals fully his emasculation. In "A Matter of Measurements," Scott confesses that Zelda has accused him of sexual inadequacy, "that the way I was built I could never make any woman happy" (190).

Hemingway's conventional notion of masculine sexual roles in *A Moveable Feast* is paralleled by an equally traditional sexual moralism. That the painter Pascin, whose work Hemingway admires, is destroying himself is apparent in Hemingway's account of him drunk in a café accompanied by two pretty models and by his allusion to Pascin's later suicide. Pascin invites Hemingway to join them for dinner and also implies that Hemingway is welcome to one of the girls. "No," replies Hemingway, "I go to eat with my *légitime*" (104). Throughout *A Moveable Feast,* Hemingway may be responding creatively to the heightened sexuality of the Paris moment, as in the scene at the "good café," but he goes home then and now to Hadley. Indeed, it is only when he stops going home to her—when, on his way from New York to Schruns (at the close of *A Moveable Feast*), he delays his journey by stopping in Paris to consummate his relationship with Pauline—that his rich and productive Paris years come to an end.

Henry Miller's remark that "rocking here in his cradle each one slips back into his soil" thus has a special relevance to Hemingway's sexual ideas in *A Moveable Feast*. For though Hemingway boldly endorses and exploits the trope of artistic potency, he casts the trope within assumptions and beliefs that would be fully acceptable in middle America. Artistic potency is associated in his mind with male heterosexuality and with a marriage partner.

Hemingway's account of writing a story at the "good café" on the place Saint-Michel contains still another major trope of expatriate autobiography. Having finished the story,

I asked the waiter for a dozen *portugaises* and a half-carafe of the dry
white wine they had there. After writing a story I was always empty and
both sad and happy, as though I had made love. . . .

As I ate the oysters with their strong taste of the sea and their faint
metallic taste that the cool white wine washed away, leaving only the
sea taste and the succulent texture, and as I drank their cold liquid from
each shell . . . , I lost the empty feeling and began to be happy and to
make plans. (6)

Hemingway here introduces one of his most pervasive tropes for the
artist's capacity for productivity in Paris, that relating to sustenance and
consumption. Of course, the young, healthy, and "natural heavyweight"
writer, who also conceives of himself as poor,[7] is seemingly pursued by
the gastronomic smells and sights of Paris on his walks through the city,
and Hemingway humorously describes, in "Hunger Was a Good Dis-
cipline," the skill necessary to negotiate a journey without stimulating
his digestive juices. But the hunger motif of *A Moveable Feast,* though
most apparent in Hemingway's need for food and drink, also encom-
passes other kinds of sustenance for the young writer seeking to write
truly and well. There is also the hunger for the books at Shakespeare
& Co. ("a great treasure" [134], he notes at one point), for the paintings
at the Luxembourg and at Stein's, and for the companionship and love
of Hadley. All these sources of physical, intellectual, and emotional
nourishment help establish what can be called a creative alimentary
process. Hunger is assuaged, which produces the capacity for creativity,
which is followed by further hunger. The process is described precisely
and in its most elementary form during the two scenes of the memoir
in which Hemingway recounts the writing of specific stories. In the
first, set in the "good café," he writes "The Three-Day Blow," and
hungry afterward, orders oysters and wine. In the second, desperately
hungry, he consumes a large meal at the Brasserie Lipp and then writes
a good portion of "Big Two-Hearted River" at the Closerie des Lilas
(72–77). The process, in short, is seemingly endless. Sustenance, and
of course sustenance not limited to food but rendered most clearly by
food, results in the capacity for work, which results in hunger, which—
once satisfied—again produces the capacity for work. And since Paris

7. Tavernier-Courbin (*Ernest Hemingway's "A Moveable Feast,"* 91–92) points out that the
Hemingways were not really poor in Paris, since Hadley's legacy paid them three thousand dollars
a year, a considerable sum in the early 1920s. But Hemingway later always depicted himself as
poor during this stage of his career.

bountifully offers up every form of nourishment—the delicious and plentiful and cheap food and wine, the rich store of books at the rue de L'Odéon, the new Mirós to hand, the warmth and support of a Hadley or a Sylvia Beach or an Ezra Pound—the work flows forth fully and finely in a kind of creative alchemy in which, to reverse the biblical formula, the flesh becomes the word.

Hemingway links two major themes to this central trope of the capacity of Paris to nourish the artist. The first, present throughout *A Moveable Feast,* is that Paris is a place to work, not to play. Hemingway is shocked when Fitzgerald, unable to work, "laid the failure to Paris, the town best organized for a writer to write in that there is" (182). What Hemingway means by *organized* is that he has shaped his own life into a circuit of nourishment and productivity. Most daytime hours are carefully hoarded—especially after January, 1924, when the Hemingways return to Paris with their child—for the slow process of writing and rewriting, and anything distracting him from or interfering with this activity must be resisted. Hemingway describes in some detail, in "The End of an Avocation," the seductive appeal of race handicapping, which he resists finally, "because it took too much time, I was getting too involved" (62). And he describes his resentment on several occasions when his workplace sanctuary, the Closerie des Lilas, is invaded by outsiders or threatened with change by the installation of an "American bar."

Hemingway of course devoted much effort throughout his career to cultivating a sometimes self-serving image of the commitment and pain necessary in pursuit of the writer's craft. But whatever doubts there might be about the actual amount of time Hemingway devoted to his literary labors during his early Paris years, the *idea* of work functions successfully as a literary construct in *A Moveable Feast.* The sketches, in their various ways, present an account of a young writer drawing strength and inspiration from his surroundings while resisting their sapping blandishments, and thereby achieving the skill necessary to produce *In Our Time* and *The Sun Also Rises.* Hemingway's work ethic in *A Moveable Feast* functions much like the trope of artistic potency in that both reveal how an American writer can at once draw upon the distinctive beneficial attributes of a foreign culture and yet retain his distinctive American values. The avid consumer of Turgenev novels borrowed from Shakespeare & Co. and of Cézannes viewed at the Musée du Luxembourg was also anxious to return home to his wife and child and was contemptuous toward the bohemian wastrels and sexual "misfits" of Montparnasse.

The second major theme that Hemingway links to the trope of Paris' capacity to satisfy the artist's hunger is that of luck. Hemingway describes himself in *A Moveable Feast* as someone who practices many of the conventional artifices for placating fate. He carries a rabbit's foot and will knock on wood to ward off misfortune. But he also connects the idea of luck to the hunger motif. Several times during the work he and Hadley congratulate themselves on their good luck in being young and happy and living and working in Paris. In addition, they are often lucky at the track, though Hemingway is quick to note that skill and inside information also help in picking winners.

All these themes come together in the sketch "A False Spring." Hemingway and Hadley have won at the races, and after some seafood at an expensive restaurant they walk through the heart of Paris reminiscing about the good fortune they have experienced since arriving in Europe. They pause on a bridge over the Seine. "We looked and there it all was: our river and our city and the island of our city. 'We're too lucky,' she said" (55). They are hungry again and examine a menu outside a restaurant.

> Standing there I wondered how much of what we had felt on the bridge was just hunger. I asked my wife and she said, "I don't know, Tatie. There are so many sorts of hunger. In the spring there are more. But that's gone now. Memory is hunger."
>
> I was being stupid, and looking in the window and seeing two *tournedos* being served I knew I was hungry in a simple way.
>
> "You said we were lucky today. Of course we were. But we had very good advice and information."
>
> She laughed.
>
> "I didn't mean about the racing. You're such a literal boy. I meant lucky other ways." (56–57)

They have a "wonderful meal," but afterward,

> the feeling that had been like hunger when we were on the bridge was still there. . . . It was there when we came in the room and after we had gone to bed and made love in the dark, it was there. . . . I had to try to think it out and I was too stupid. Life had seemed so simple that morning. . . . But Paris was a very old city and we were young and nothing was simple there, not even poverty, nor sudden money, nor the moonlight, nor right and wrong nor the breathing of someone who lay beside you in the moonlight. (57–58)

Hemingway is asking us, in this sketch, to view his and Hadley's happiness in the context of time as time is expressed within the motifs of hunger and luck. All life seems simple and literal to Hemingway initially, because he is living in the present. He has won at the races and is therefore lucky, and he has had his hunger assuaged by a good meal. Hadley's comments that "memory is hunger" and that she meant "lucky in other ways" disturb and confuse him because he is still "too stupid" to understand her recognition and acceptance of mutability—that the freshness and excitement of youth, of living in the "moonlight," will pass, leaving the hunger of memories (that is, a desire for the good life of the past) and a realization that to be happy, given that all things change, is to be lucky. Paris, as a "very old city," is the proper setting for this interplay between the innocence of youth (Hemingway's role) and the wisdom of experience (Hadley's role). Eventually, of course, Hemingway will enter the world of experiential knowledge and will act out fully, in the writing of *A Moveable Feast,* his hunger for the lucky days of the past.

The interrelated motifs of sustenance (including the work theme) and luck reach a tragic climax in the conclusion of *A Moveable Feast,* set in Schruns, with Hemingway's earlier characterization of himself as an innocent playing a large role in the climax. Schruns is in one sense a surrogate for Paris, since it is an excellent place to work on the criteria Hemingway has established in connection with Paris. There is much good food and drink, pleasant companionship, and Hadley. In its isolation as a mountain town in winter it is also a kind of private Eden, seemingly timeless and inviolate in its routine of writing, skiing, eating, reading, and lovemaking. It constitutes, in brief, a "happy and inno-cent" place and moment (207). But "during our last year in the moun-tains new people came deep into our lives and nothing was ever the same again" (207). These interlopers—not named by Hemingway—are the "pilot fish" John Dos Passos and two others he guides, Sara and Gerald Murphy. The Murphys are a more ingratiating variation on the fashionable literati surrounding Pound whom Hemingway had eluded in Paris. But now, reassured by Dos Passos, he allows himself to be praised and taken up by them and thus finds himself, in his "inexpe-rience"(208), drawn into the orbit of the idle rich whose sycophantic clinging and whose jealous interruption of the pattern of hunger and creativity break the productive circuit of the writer in luck. And he succumbs, only to discover that the rich, "when they have passed and taken the nourishment they needed, leave everything deader than the roots of any grass Attila's horses' hooves have ever scoured" (208).

This ravaging of the writer's landscape of creative fertility is completed by another rich "infiltrator" (209), the charming young woman Pauline Pfeiffer—also not named—who in the role of companion to the often neglected Hadley makes herself desirable to Hemingway. "The husband has two attractive girls around when he has finished work. One is new and strange and if he has bad luck he gets to love them both" (210). In one sense, of course, Hemingway's use of *luck* in this instance can be viewed as an effort to dodge his personal responsibility for becoming involved with Pauline. But the term also relates, in the context of its earlier usage, to the theme of the inevitability of change in human affairs and especially to the transitory character of happiness. "Luck" is to possess happiness, "bad luck" is to see the happy moment pass.

Hemingway consummates his relationship with Pauline later that winter in Paris, on his way back from New York to Schruns, but once he has returned to Schruns he and Hadley are temporarily reunited. "I worked well and we made great trips, and I thought we were invulnerable again, and it wasn't until we were out of the mountains in late spring, and back in Paris that the other thing started again" (211). With this fall from innocence, "Paris was never to be the same again" (211). The Paris that Hemingway creates before his fall is thus a kind of writer's Eden in which the city's capacity to nourish his creative potency is richly productive. But his moment of luck is susceptible to time and thus change, with the idle rich and the seductive woman the agents of a fall from the innocence of a pure work ethic and a pure sexuality. Paris can never be the same, Hemingway concludes, because he himself has changed. He has become less the American innocent he was and more the bohemian expatriate he had resisted becoming. And this, to his mind, is a fall from grace.

Hemingway's account of his maturation within the Paris moment—of hunger assuaged, potency achieved, and luck in place—is especially open to objection for its portraits of his contemporaries. Duplicating to a degree the furor that greeted Stein's recollections of her friends in *The Autobiography of Alice B. Toklas,* when a number of them banded together to publish "Testimony Against Gertrude Stein," the partisans of almost all the figures negatively portrayed in *A Moveable Feast* have hastened to specify the inaccuracies and distortions in Hemingway's accounts.[8] Much of this criticism, though well intentioned in its resolve to set the record straight, is beside the point. *A Moveable Feast* seeks to express a mythic Paris of creative fertility. One way that Hemingway chose to achieve this end was to shape his Paris experiences around tropes of sustenance and potency. Another was to polarize his expatriate contemporaries into those figures who contributed, by their aid and example, to his development and those who provided at most instructive instances of a failure to develop "in the town best organized for a writer to write in that there is" (182). Viewed in this light, Hemingway's "distortions" resemble those of a cubist painter. Just as *A Moveable Feast* is cubist or spatial in the sense that each of its sketches functions less in relation to its chronological siting in the narrative than to its contribution to a vision of the Paris moment as a whole, so its character portraits follow the cubist tendency toward distortion of the superficial appearance of an object in order to abstract the essence of the object's shape. And for Hemingway—as for Henry Miller, too, in the caricature of his friends in *Tropic of Cancer*—the essence of the people he knew in Paris lay in the relationship of each figure to a mythic Paris of sustenance and potency. Those who played a positive role within this myth reached almost angelic status; those who did not were reduced to devils. Portraits of this kind are not true in any biographical sense, just as a cubist portrait is not a realistic likeness of its subject. They are, however, a form of abstract or intellectualized truth in their intimate relationship to a mythic Paris of creativity.

Angels are far less common than devils among Hemingway's portraits. Chief among the angels is Hadley, who falls into a category of feminine characterization familiar to anyone who reads Hemingway. *A Moveable Feast* makes occasional reference to her life apart from Hemingway's— her piano playing, for example, or her concern about adequate clothing—but otherwise she is described entirely in relation to the supportive role she plays vis-à-vis Hemingway's moods and needs. A characteristic note is struck in the opening sketch, when Hemingway returns from the "good café" with plans to escape the ugly and cold early winter of Paris for the mountains.

---

8. Tavernier-Courbin (*Ernest Hemingway's "A Moveable Feast,"* 65–98) notes the attacks and seeks to distinguish between "fact and fiction" in Hemingway's accounts. "Testimony Against Gertrude Stein" was published as a supplement to the July, 1935, issue of the Paris-based journal *Transition*. It included responses by, among others, Georges Braque, Henri Matisse, and Eugene Jolas.

"I think it would be wonderful, Tatie," my wife said. She had a gently modeled face and her eyes and her smile lighted up at decisions as though they were rich presents. "When should we leave?"

"Whenever you want."

"Oh, I want to right away. Didn't you know?"

"Maybe it will be fine and clear when we come back. It can be very fine when it is clear and cold."

"I am sure it will be," she said. "Weren't you good to think of going, too." (7–8)

The "rich presents" that Hadley finds in Hemingway's proposals constitute a firm foundation of support for the young artist. She and he travel together and go to the races together, she is at home with meals when he has finished work, and she is warmly present in bed in the moonlight. Missing entirely from the picture of Hadley in *A Moveable Feast* are Hemingway's anxiety about living on Hadley's money (an almost psychopathic obsession about rich women supporting artists that was to plague him all his life), his fears about her becoming pregnant, and—after the birth of their child—his irritation over the child's distracting effect on their relationship. (A good many of these concerns are evident, however, in the marriage stories of *In Our Time*.) In the failure to give a fully accurate account of his relationship to Hadley, Hemingway was in *A Moveable Feast* reconstructing his marriage not only under the powerful impulse of a combined sense of guilt and nostalgia but also in order to portray it, within his nurturing and potency motifs, as one of the most important sources of the artist's development. All must be well at home for the writer, in short, with *well* a measurement of the degree of support by the writer's wife. Fitzgerald and Zelda's marriage, in which Zelda's jealousy toward Scott undermines his ability to work, of course offers the most instructive contrast to that of Hemingway and Hadley. But Stein's sexual submissiveness to Toklas and Pascin's sexual excesses, both of which are depicted as keys to their weakness or self-destructiveness as artists, also inform Hemingway's theme that the American artist in Paris is most successful when he maintains a "normal" American marriage.

Hemingway is equally selective in his portrayal of Sylvia Beach. Although Beach was a lesbian, Hemingway is notably silent on this aspect of her life, one that he depicts negatively in connection with other figures in *A Moveable Feast*. He is content to let us see Beach as a mixture of surrogate mother and surrogate wife. She, like Hadley, is

Shakespeare & Co. Sylvia Beach (center), with James Joyce and Adrienne Monnier.
Sylvia Beach Papers, Box 277, Folder 8, Manuscripts Division, Department of Rare Books and Special Collections, Princeton University Libraries. Used by permission.

concerned about his physical well-being, including whether he is getting enough to eat. But whereas Hadley offers sexual comfort, Beach provides intellectual nutriment through the books of Shakespeare & Co.

Far more common in *A Moveable Feast* are figures who in their personal or artistic lives exemplify a failure to respond to what Paris has to offer the artist and thereby serve as negative models for the aspiring artist. These exemplars of the false or inadequate range from Ford Madox Ford, in his empty self-importance, and Ernest Walsh, in his con man's literary sharp dealing, to Cheever Dunning, with his opium habit, and Evan Shipman, with his alcoholism. Paris is full of phonies and failures, in other words, and it behooves the serious writer to stay clear of the first and to avoid the excesses of the second. Considerably more complex, however, in their role as negative models, are the portraits of Stein, Pound, and Fitzgerald.

Stein initially appears in a favorable light within the sustenance trope. When Hemingway and Hadley call on Stein in early 1922, "she and the friend who lived with her had been very cordial and friendly and we had loved the big studio with the great paintings. It was like one of the best rooms in the finest museum except there was a big fireplace and it was warm and comfortable and they gave you good things to eat" (13–14). Hemingway's favorite images for the nurturing available in Paris—warmth, food, and art—are here joined in a single scene. What is more, Stein, by emphasizing verbal purity and sentence rhythm in her own writing, was working in a direction toward which Hemingway was instinctively sympathetic, and he therefore at first responded positively to her comments and suggestions about his writing. But gradually, as his portrait of her moves through the three sketches it comprises, Stein's weaknesses and limitations begin to predominate. In the end, she emerges, along with Fitzgerald, as the book's principal example of the flawed or wounded talent whose work and life exhibit what the writer must avoid in order to write well and truly. Stein's major weaknesses, aside from her irritating habit of wishing to instruct Hemingway in areas of life in which she has little experience, is an overconcern with the popular acceptance of her work, notwithstanding her commitment to the radically new, and a disinclination to expend the effort to revise carefully. These flaws are, to Hemingway, symptomatic of her deficient toughness of mind, and it is therefore not surprising that he concludes his portrait with the scene in which she shows abject sexual submissiveness to her "wife," Alice Toklas.

The three sketches of Fitzgerald, toward the close of *A Moveable Feast,* hammer in this theme. Fitzgerald, like Stein, is depicted as a major talent with major flaws. Encumbered by an expensive apartment on the Right Bank, a car, and servants, he is dependent on selling his stories to popular magazines and feels little compunction about revising his stories to suit the market. (Both Stein and Fitzgerald mention the *Saturday Evening Post* as an outlet they would welcome for their work.) Like Stein's essential weakness of character, Fitzgerald's is clearly tied to sexual submission—though with him it is represented as well by a compulsion to drink despite his awareness of a susceptibility to alcohol. Indeed, Hemingway fashions his picture of Fitzgerald into an almost exact foil for his own attributes within the sustenance and potency tropes of *A Moveable Feast.* Fitzgerald has little knowledge or appreciation of food, no capacity to drink, is not interested in the potential riches of French art and life, and is constantly subverted rather than supported by Zelda.

Hemingway's negative portraits of his fellow expatriates in *A Moveable Feast* often stem from ill feeling toward them as a result of later events in their relationship and his projection of his rancor onto the past in the service of the central themes of the work. Stein's characterization of Hemingway as a Rotarian in *The Autobiography of Alice B. Toklas,* his bitter political quarrel with Dos Passos during the 1930s, and the resentment he felt over Fitzgerald's rediscovery in the 1950s all underlie his depiction of these figure in *A Moveable Feast.*[9] Nowhere is the impact of the more recent past on the account of an earlier moment more apparent than in Hemingway's portrayal of Pound. Pound, we learn, is a man of warm sympathies and strong loyalties but of little judgment. He is a good friend to Hemingway, but he has also gathered under his wing Wyndham Lewis: "I do not think I had ever seen a nastier-looking man" (109). Pound is "masculine" in his enthusiasm for tennis and boxing but is also active in Natalie Barney's lesbian-centered Bel Esprit projects, including an attempt to come to the financial aid of T. S. Eliot. The ambivalent verdict on him is of course related to Hemingway's contempt for homosexuality within the potency trope of *A Moveable Feast,* but it is also deeply colored by his awareness of Pound's efforts during the 1930s and 1940s in behalf of Italian fascism. (It is significant that in "Ezra Pound and His Bel Esprit," Hemingway links Pound, Eliot, and Lewis, the three principal Anglo-American fascist sympathizers of the 1930s.) Pound, Hemingway seems to be saying, was a positive force during the 1920s in Paris because of his masculine energy and supportive nature, but his weaknesses in judgment were already apparent.

In *A Moveable Feast,* Hemingway not only sharply tilted his portraits of his fellow expatriates to conform with the central tropes of the work but also polarized his characterization of Paris settings to achieve a similar effect. Broadly speaking, Hemingway subscribed to the platitude that young artists are better off in garrets than in palaces. In Paris, the most productive places to live and work are his simple Contrescarpe rooms and his nearby cheap, cold, and bare studio on the rue Mouffetard, his noisy apartment over a sawmill on the rue Notre-Dame-des-Champs, and several remote and unpopular cafés, such as the "good café" on the place Saint-Michel and the Closerie des Lilas on the corner of the boulevard Montparnasse and the boulevard Saint-Michel. The simplicity and honesty of these milieus are the physical and social equivalents of the simplicity and honesty of Hadley's and Sylvia Beach's supportive roles in his artistic productivity. These are places where he can live and work well and truly.

9. Gertrude Stein, *The Autobiography of Alice B. Toklas* (1933; rpr. New York, 1955), 220. See Donald Pizer, "The Hemingway–Dos Passos Relationship," *Journal of Modern Literature,* XIII (1986), 111–28.

In contrast are, above all, the principal Montparnasse expatriate cafés at the boulevard Raspail end of the boulevard Montparnasse— the Rotonde, Sélect, Dôme, and Coupole—where wastrel dilettantes spend their days and nights.[10] (After Hemingway moved to the Montparnasse quartier in 1924, where he lived only a short walk from these cafés, he occasionally did stop off briefly at the least Americanized of them, the Dôme, as he does in "With Pascin at the Dôme," but only for a predinner beer after work.) Equally suspect are the studios and apartments occupied by well-to-do expatriates, such as Stein's "rich" studio (a setting for her seductive "instruction" of young writers), Fitzgerald's large Right Bank apartment, and Natalie Barney's house on the rue Jacob (a lesbian gathering place). In one sense, Hemingway is in this opposition of settings indulging in a tired cliché, one he sums up at the close of *A Moveable Feast* when he describes the book as an account of "how Paris was in the early days when we were very poor and very happy" (211). But the opposition also contributes appreciably to the underlying mythic character of the work as a whole, in which life in Paris, for the youthful aspirant to art, is a magical journey through a world populated by good and bad spirits and in which each detail of the landscape addresses the quester's capacity for hope and despair and for fortitude and weakness.

What can usefully be described as the cubist form of *A Moveable Feast* thus achieves the effect of a timeless simultaneity. People, places, and events either contribute to or detract from the growth and productivity of the artist (his sustenance and potency) and thereby create an effect of synchronic alternatives rather than of diachronic causality— of plot, in short. Nevertheless, *A Moveable Feast* also contains within this modernist spatial form a number of thematically driven forward-moving impulses.

One such impulse is apparent in the division of *A Moveable Feast* into two parts corresponding to the two phases of Hemingway's Paris moment. The first phase, that of his residence in the Contrescarpe quartier, is one of discovery and development. It is there that the tropes of sustenance and potency are given fullest play in Hemingway's discovery of a Paris of good things to eat and drink, of good places in

---

10. Hemingway's contempt for the fashionable Montparnasse cafés was almost immediate. In his dispatch "American Bohemians in Paris" to the *Toronto Star Weekly* for March 25, 1922, he wrote (after only three months in Paris), "The scum of Greenwich Village, New York, has been skimmed off and deposited in large ladles on that section of Paris adjacent to the Café Rotonde" (Ernest Hemingway, *Dateline: Toronto,* ed. William White [New York, 1985], 114).

which to work, of books and paintings, and of people concerned about his well-being and work. It is in this setting, Hemingway implies, that he comes of age as a writer. (It is significant that he misdates the composition of "The Three-Day Blow" as occurring during this period. He wrote this and almost all the stories of *In Our Time* after his return to Paris from Canada in early 1924.[11] But his error is in tune with his idea that he came to artistic maturity during the winter of 1922–1923.) The second phase of *A Moveable Feast,* however, which describes the Hemingways at rue Notre-Dame-des-Champs, is dominated by sketches that dramatize the dangers—and thus the potential for a fall, for a loss of "luck"—facing the aspiring writer in Paris. The city is revealed as swarming with phonies and poseurs (Ford, Walsh, "Hal," and Lewis) and as a setting in which good writers and artists succeed in destroying themselves (Dunning, Shipman, and Pascin). Most telling of all in expressing a sense of impending doom during this phase of Hemingway's Paris years, his most prized "good place," the Closerie des Lilas, is first invaded by a Montparnasse homosexual and then further contaminated by its owner's conversion of it into an American-style bar—an invasion and destruction of a sanctuary that anticipates the collapse of Hemingway's Eden at Schruns at the close of the book.

The tonal difference in the two parts of *A Moveable Feast* is reflected in the major portraits of each of the parts. Stein, as depicted soon after Hemingway's arrival in Paris, though revealing flaws in character and insight, contributes to Hemingway's development through her interest in him and his writing. Fitzgerald, however, who makes his appearance later in the work, contributes nothing to Hemingway's career.[12] On the contrary, Fitzgerald's capitulation to the crippling effects of money and sex—images of illness and death pervade the portrayal of Fitzgerald—looks forward to Hemingway's own fall before the combined assault of the idle rich and the sexual adventurer in the sketch immediately following the final sketch of Fitzgerald.

Hemingway's account in *A Moveable Feast* of his artistic growth and personal loss during his Paris years is a variation on the myth of the fortunate fall. The young and innocent writer seeks knowledge and power (or sustenance and potency) in the creative Eden that is Paris. He gains these but suffers as well the loss of his happiness and his Eden.

---

11. See Paul Smith, *A Reader's Guide to the Short Stories of Ernest Hemingway* (Boston, 1989).

12. It is significant in this context that Hemingway omits any reference to Fitzgerald's important participation in the revision of *The Sun Also Rises* in early 1926.

The image of a lost Eden is one of the most evocative and permanent resources of the western imagination, with writers and artists drawing upon a host of symbolic equivalents of the journey from innocence and bliss to tragic knowledge. For Hemingway, Paris served this role well.

Gertrude Stein
The Autobiography of Alice B. Toklas

The Autobiography of Alice B. Toklas appears to be a disarmingly accessible work. Its anecdotal form, chatty tone, and generous offering of witty and often catty commentary contributed to its immediate popularity as well as to its continuing reputation as the most charming and readable of Stein's works. Stein herself had a hand in establishing the reputation of the *Autobiography* as a pleasant but lightweight reminiscence through her accounts of the speed of its composition and her remark, at the close of the work, that she had attempted to write the *Autobiography* "as simply as Defoe did the Autobiography of Robinson Crusoe."[1] A moment's reflection reminds us, though, that Stein always wrote very quickly, whatever the complexity or indirection of what she was attempting to express, and that *Robinson Crusoe* is an exceedingly dense and rich work despite its appearance of a simple tale simply told. Indeed, so central is the seemingly ingenuous form of *The Autobiography of Alice B. Toklas* in communicating Stein's interpretation of her life as an American artist in Paris that it is useful to adopt the old-fashioned—but often still rewarding—critical method of approaching the themes of the work through aspects of its technique and structure.[2]

1. Gertrude Stein, *The Autobiography of Alice B. Toklas* (1933; rpr. New York, 1955), 252. Further citations of this edition will appear in the text. For biographical information about Stein, I have relied principally on Richard Bridgman's *Gertrude Stein in Pieces* (New York, 1970) and James R. Mellow's *Charmed Circle: Gertrude Stein and Company* (New York, 1974). In addition, Shari Benstock (*Women of the Left Bank: Paris, 1900–1940* [Austin, Tex., 1986], 143–93) discusses Stein and Toklas in the context of other Paris lesbian relationships, and Diana Souhami's *Gertrude and Alice* (London, 1991) is a sympathetic biography dealing with the relationship between Stein and Toklas.

2. Discussions of form and technique in Stein's work generally slight the *Autobiography* in favor of her more obviously experimental works. But see Lynn Z. Bloom, "Gertrude Is Alice Is Everybody: Innovation and Point of View in Gertrude Stein's Autobiographies," *Twentieth Century*

The most striking characteristic of the form of the *Autobiography* is Stein's decision to recount her own life in the voice of Toklas. (By *voice,* I mean both Toklas' point of view and her mannerisms of expression. Those who knew Toklas have often commented on how closely Stein approximates her manner of speech.) The choice of this narrative point of view plays a number of obvious roles. The transparent "hoax" of authorship—the first edition did not list an author on the title page—confirms the work's lightness. But adopting Toklas' point of view also enables Stein to declare openly, with seeming objectivity, the significance of her own role in the formation of modernism and the worth of her own writing. A focus on these functions, however, obscures the fact that the union of Stein's authorship and Toklas' voice in a single narrative presence constitutes a powerful metaphor for the "marriage" of the two figures for the greater portion of their lives. Stein and Toklas, unlike many of the expatriate lesbian couples of Paris, did not flaunt their relationship. And nowhere in the *Autobiography* is there any hint of passion or sexuality in the account of their years together at 27 rue de Fleurus. But their union is announced and celebrated in the tour de force of absorbing Toklas' life and voice into Stein's account of her own life.

This achievement, in part because of its seamless unity of tone, mirrors not only a union but an ideal union—a true marriage of two different but ideally complementary temperaments and talents.[3] In recounting Toklas' early life, in the first chapter, Stein at once establishes Toklas' role as the feminine principle in a productive relationship. Toklas is interested in reading, gardening, and the arts, and she abhors violence. Later, as a full partner in successfully running 27 rue de Fleurus as a center of radical art, with Stein as its leading exponent in prose, she tends to the necessary household and secretarial tasks.[4] Stein, on the other hand, fills the masculine role of thinker and creator and is the active force in their lives. In an often-repeated and therefore heavily symbolic realization of a gender-controlled concept of perfect comple-

---

Literature, XXIV (1978), 81–93; and Shirley C. Neuman, *Gertrude Stein: Autobiography and the Problem of Narration* (Victoria, B.C., 1979), 21–32.

3. Catharine R. Stimpson ("Gertrice/Altrude: Stein, Toklas, and the Paradox of the Happy Marriage," in *Mothering the Mind,* ed. Ruth Perry and Martine W. Brownley [New York, 1984], 122–39) provides an interpretation of the relationship between Stein and Toklas as a form of marriage, but she discusses the *Autobiography* only in passing.

4. In marking Toklas' arrival in Paris in 1907 as the beginning of their relationship, Stein obscures the fact that Toklas did not join her at 27 rue de Fleurus until 1909 and that Leo Stein continued to live there until 1913.

mentarity, when guests are entertained at rue de Fleurus, Stein talks to the artist and Toklas to the wife of the artist. And when, later in the *Autobiography,* Stein and Toklas acquire a car, Stein drives and Toklas is driven.

It can be argued that because it is Stein who is articulating this notion of an ideal harmony, the *Autobiography* paradoxically confirms a traditional male perspective in which the man finds perfection because he is playing the fulfilling roles of dominance at home and active participation in the world's affairs outside the home. (Stein's absorption, or "consumption," of Toklas' character into the narrative voice of the *Autobiography* can also be interpreted as a typically male use of the female.) Stein, I believe, is aware of this possibility and on several occasions refers to Toklas' good-natured chafing under the limitations of the feminine role even while fully accepting the role. For example, at the opening of Chapter 3, "1907–1914," Stein has Toklas write, "As I said Fernande [Picasso's companion] was the first wife of a genius I was to sit with. The geniuses came and talked to Gertrude Stein and the wives sat with me. How they unroll, an endless vista through the years" (87).

Still, it is necessary to stress that Stein's intent in using Toklas' voice—and to a great extent as well its effect—was to dramatize Toklas' significant role in Stein's performance of her own dual heroic roles as discoverer and champion of pictorial modernism and as practitioner and aesthetician of literary modernism. In this regard, the *Autobiography* is a kind of sentimental domestic novel. Stein and Toklas meet, decide to join their lives, and then live happily ever after in their charming house on the rue de Fleurus, where they entertain many interesting artists and writers. The frontispiece photograph of the first edition of the *Autobiography* renders this domestic image.[5] The photograph, by Man Ray, shows Stein writing at her desk in the large single-room atelier adjoining their living quarters as Toklas is entering the door. The artist is at work—work that also includes the masculine job of speaking for the two of them in the *Autobiography.* The artist's companion and aide temporarily joins her, no doubt on some domestic errand. The underlying but never explicit theme of *The Autobiography of Alice B. Toklas* is that it is largely the happy and successful "marriage" of Gertrude and Alice that has permitted Stein to pursue her triumphant career. The

5. Unfortunately, modern reprints of the *Autobiography* omit the sixteen photographs Stein selected for the first edition.

Toklas at the door, Stein at her desk, in the frontispiece of *The Autobiography of Alice B. Toklas*
Photograph by Man Ray. © 1995 Artists Rights Society (ARS), New York/ADAGP/Man Ray Trust,
Paris.

Autobiography has often been misunderstood by casual readers as egotistical because of Stein's frequent comments on her own importance. It has not been realized that such remarks are a form of love letter to Toklas, whose domestic skills, companionship, and love have made possible the full flowering of Stein's creative powers.

Toklas and Stein in the atelier at 27 rue de Fleurus
Photograph by Man Ray. © 1995 Artists Rights Society (ARS), New York/ADAGP/Man Ray Trust, Paris.

What at first seems a radical sexual theme thus pervades the *Autobiography.* Although Stein appears to accept the premise that she and Toklas share a love that dare not speak its name, the narrative form of the *Autobiography,* as a symbolic expression of their union, declares and celebrates their love. But as with Hemingway's sexual themes in *A Moveable Feast* and (it will be seen) *The Sun Also Rises,* a deeply conservative ethic accompanies and ultimately reshapes the ostensible radical sexuality. Thus, in the manner of Hemingway's "good café" scene in *A Moveable Feast,* sexuality and creativity join in the *Autobiography* in ways in which the image of union relies on the sexual but which subsume the sexual under the artistic expression that is the permanent and significant product of the union—as, for example, when Stein and Toklas are joined in Man Ray's frontispiece but Stein is occupied with her writing. Moreover, the locus of the union, the *pavillon* and atelier at 27 rue de Fleurus, is both a center of artistic creativity and a home in the traditional meaning of the word—that is, a setting where conventional middle-class male and female roles are played out within a nineteenth-century model of marital domesticity. The solid German-Jewish values of productive labor within a family-based culture which had been Stein's "womb" or "soil"—to return to Miller's metaphors of one's national roots—are only partly disguised by the aura of the new and radical in the lesbian relationship and artists' salon of 27 rue de Fleurus.

Another formal feature of the *Autobiography* with a decided bearing on the expression of the work's themes arises from Stein's modernist effort to mimic in its narrative method several of the ways in which the mind works.[6] At one point in the book, Stein notes that during the summer of 1913, while on a visit to Spain, her focus as a writer shifted from an interest "in the insides of people, their character and what went on inside of them," to a "desire to express the rhythm of the visible world" (119). The *Autobiography,* though written some years after this change in focus, can be seen as Stein's last major bid to get at experience from the inside—or to put the matter more formalistically, to render dramatically through specific formal strategies mental processes that are strongly linked to temperament and character. Her attempt, despite its incongruity with the kind of writing she was turning to in the 1930s, has a certain appropriateness for the *Autobiography*. The book is, after all, a retrospective work; much of it deals with Stein's career and with Stein and Toklas' life together before Stein shifted her interest to the "visible world." Its chronological moment makes a return to the narrative method she practiced during that moment acceptable and appropriate. But an even firmer basis for finding it appropriate lies in the relationship between her choice of narrative voice and what can be called her epistemological form. If the work is in large measure a testament to the importance of Toklas in Stein's life, what better way to testify to that than to imitate Toklas' thought processes in the narrative style of the work?

The *Autobiography* discloses two levels of epistemological mimicry. So far as the narrative form reflects the general operation of mental processes, it connects with Stein's experiments in automatic writing, which began at Harvard and continued through *Three Lives* and *The Making of Americans.* But the *Autobiography* seeks also to reflect the specific consciousness of Alice B. Toklas. The two principal forms of dramatic

---

6. Like most commentators on the *Autobiography,* I will cite Stein as the author of specific passages unless the discussion requires that I name Toklas as the ostensible author.

representation of consciousness in the *Autobiography*—how we come to know something, and how we later recall what we have come to know—thus render both general human mental characteristics and, in their highly charged particularity, the distinctive consciousness of Alice B. Toklas.

The lengthy introductory portion of the *Autobiography,* incorporating the first four chapters from "Before I Came to Paris" through "Gertrude Stein Before She Came to Paris," is an expression of epistemological form. Stein initially has Toklas tell us something about her life before meeting Stein in Paris. The second chapter, "My Arrival in Paris," is a much fuller account, because it introduces us to the principal object of Toklas' knowledge in the *Autobiography:* Gertrude Stein. After meeting Stein, in 1907, Toklas presumably comes to know something of her acquaintance' earlier life, first of her more immediate past (Chapter 3, "Gertrude Stein in Paris, 1903–1907") and then of her years in America (Chapter 4, "Gertrude Stein Before She Came to Paris"). We seem to come to know Stein as Toklas herself did, beginning with an impression and then deepening and extending our knowledge into Stein's life in the past.[7] But as we might realize after a moment's reflection, Toklas' fuller knowledge of Stein could only have occurred in the years following their initial meeting; it could not have been almost coexistent with the meeting, as the sequence of chapters in the *Autobiography* implies. And yet, so convincing has the writer's imitation of the knowing process been in these early chapters that Stein can proceed in Chapter 5, "1907–1914," to an account of their life together at 27 rue de Fleurus which assumes, as we assume, that Toklas has the knowledge she is represented as having acquired in Chapters 3 and 4. To put the matter another way, Stein by her ordering of the early chapters is both mirroring a process of coming to know an individual (from an immediate impression to the knowledge of a life) and playing upon the reader's assumptions (that what is presented first comes first in time) to lead him to accept her account of this process.

Stein's narrative style in the *Autobiography* mimics as well the associational nature of consciousness, which is especially conspicuous in Toklas' habitual manner of thinking. Toklas, it seems, cannot describe an event without recalling a great deal—the background of those engaged in the event, for example, or the nature of other similar events—which

---

7. This narrative device resembles the one that Fitzgerald employed for Nick's account of his knowledge of Gatsby in *The Great Gatsby* (1925), a novel Stein much admired.

appears extraneous to the event itself. The narrative is interrupted, often for some length, while the tangential is pursued. There then follows a variation on one of the most pervasive narrative bridges in the *Autobiography:* "But to come back to . . ." The associational component of consciousness confronts us from the earliest pages of the work. At the opening of Chapter 2, "My Arrival in Paris," Toklas begins to tell of her momentous full entrance into Stein's life, on the occasion of being invited to a Saturday-evening dinner party at the rue de Fleurus, which is to be followed by a larger gathering in the atelier. At the conclusion of the paragraph in which she first mentions this event, she adds, "The dinner was cooked by Hélène. I must tell a little about Hélène" (7). The little she must tell comes to three long paragraphs that go into Hélène's life both before and after the dinner party. Only then does the narrative return to the evening of Toklas' first visit: "But to come back to 1907" (8).

Stein's decision to represent the associational in her narrative structure has affinities with the resurgence in the early twentieth century of the supposition that objective reality, of actuality outside consciousness, is an intellectual and social construct dictated by convenience—that all that is known is indissolubly a part of the process of knowing, that is, of the consciousness of the knower.[8] Toklas thus relates events not only by means of her own associational recall but also with a chronological vagueness and inexactitude that accords with the belief that past events exist within the consciousness in a timeless mix—what Bergson calls, in a somewhat different context, the *durée.* In Toklas' process of recall, past events seem to float free of clock time. One event or person recalls others, and all are revealed to us within the timelessness of the act of recollection rather than as having an existence within a fixed temporal sequence. Along with "But to come back to . . . ," a common narrative bridge in the *Autobiography* is "About that time . . ."

These two large-scale instances of imitative form which I have been discussing—the coalescing of Stein and Toklas into a single narrative voice in order to express their essential oneness, and the reliance on an associational and atemporal narrative style in order to display Toklas' consciousness in operation—are closely related to yet another way of addressing the stylistic modernism of the *Autobiography,* its character as an imitation in prose of cubist form in painting. Here, too, there is a

---

8. See Stephen Kern, *The Culture of Time and Space, 1880–1918* (Cambridge, Mass., 1983), 10–64.

close connection between form and theme. Throughout the *Autobiography,* Stein underscores not only what she has done as a promoter of modernism in painting but also how she has appropriated its underlying principles for her prose. She likens her push toward a cubist form in *Three Lives* to the work of Cézanne (33–34), she sets Picasso's breakthrough to a cubist technique while he is completing her portrait alongside her own experiments in *The Making of Americans* (56–57), and she perceives herself as united with Picasso in a joint effort to create an art based on "elemental abstraction" (64).

Exactly how Stein's work, including the *Autobiography,* relates to cubism is a much discussed, complex, and still obscure subject.[9] Nevertheless, I would like to suggest two ways. First, if one of the cardinal aims of a cubist painting, at least in the initial analytic stage of the movement—the stage that mattered to Stein in the *Autobiography*—is to bring various angles of perceiving an object into a single simultaneous vision (as in a cubist portrait that superimposes one on another the different geometric shapes that the different angles of vision present), then Stein's joining of Toklas and herself in a single point of view amounts to the pursuit of that cardinal aim of cubism in narrative prose. In the *Autobiography,* two consciousnesses join in a single act of recollection, just as in a cubist painting multiple angles of vision converge in a single visual apprehension.

Second, the works of analytic cubism (principally the paintings of Picasso and Braque between 1910 and 1912) aim to represent time as well as space. By combining several angles of vision in one painting, the artist is in effect rendering several moments in time—the time necessary to move the perceiving eye of the viewer from angle to angle—as a single moment in space. The cubist painter has overturned the conventional barrier between the depiction of time and the depiction of space—the convention which held that some arts are spatial, others temporal—and has also suggested the artificiality of the conventional notion of the absolutes of clock time by rendering two moments of time as simultaneously existent in the consciousness of the perceiver of an object. Stein's epistemological and associational narrative styles in the *Autobiography* can be considered an approximation, in prose, of the cubist emphasis on consciousness in the rendering of time. By having

9. See especially Wendy Steiner, "Literary Cubism: The Limits of the Analogy," in *Exact Resemblance to Exact Resemblance: The Literary Portraiture of Gertrude Stein* (New Haven, 1978), 131–60.

Toklas tell the story of her life with Stein as a process of coming to know Stein and as an associational body of recollection, Stein breaks away from the notion that an event or object exists as an independent entity and accepts instead the cubist assumption that the consciousness of the perceiver determines both the method of perceiving and what is perceived.

The final stylistic characteristic of the *Autobiography* that I will discuss is its anecdotal narrative structure. This is so pronounced that the impression of most casual readers is that the work is little more than an assemblage of brief anecdotes, loosely connected, about the very talented but often wayward artists, writers, and friends who frequented 27 rue de Fleurus. A typical anecdotal block is built around an event, whether an extended and extraordinary occasion such as the Rousseau banquet or Stein and Toklas' first visit to Belignin, or merely the first visit of someone to the rue de Fleurus. It often includes a seemingly digressive account of the background and temperament of the figure who is the focus of the anecdote, a record of some of the piquant conversational exchanges, and an emphatic closure in the form of a final witty remark or a bit of dramatic action. A transition to the next anecdotal block will be made by a characteristic "But to come back to . . ." or "About that time . . ."

Although this anecdotal narrative form is appealing, in that it is often amusing and seldom taxes the reader, it does run the risk of superficiality. This is all very pleasant, the reader is apt to feel, but how are Stein's claims to greatness, made in asides, supported by the form she has chosen for telling of her life? The answer to this question, a response that also speaks to the holding power and importance of the *Autobiography* as an expatriate work, resides in several of the basic characteristics of Stein's anecdotal method.

One way in which the anecdotal form of the *Autobiography* aggrandizes Stein's significance in the rise of modernism lies in the role she plays in the amusing accounts of the figures she meets and comes to know. It has often been remarked that her anecdotal portraits of the great artists in her circle—Picasso, for example, or Matisse, Apollinaire, or Hemingway—reduce each figure to the level of an inspired but petulant child.[10] We are informed of the particular artist's significance or greatness, but the stories told about him center on his greed, pride, envy, or self-centeredness, always within a petty context. For example,

10. See, for example, Bridgman, *Gertrude Stein in Pieces,* 222.

Stein tells the story of a breakup between Picasso and Fernande not as an event of emotional and artistic significance for Picasso—Fernande, after all, was his first great love—but as a vignette in which the two of them argue over who will first get to see the Sunday comics that Stein had earlier brought to them jointly (25–26). Fernande and Picasso do behave childishly, as portrayed in the anecdote, in extending their quarrel into the trivialities of life. Stein, however, remains serene and conciliatory and seeks to resolve the problem. She is the adult—or, to employ a perhaps more useful term for her role in the development of modernism, the mother. Hers is the household, the home, in the rue de Fleurus. Others come to her for explanations, advice, and support, but she seldom ventures into the homes of others. Within her anecdotal form, she serves as a permanent center of common sense, stability, and order, whether her strength and good sense are overt, as in the case of the Sunday comics, or rendered only tonally, by the difference between the dispassionate teller of the anecdote—a teller who of course melds Stein and Toklas in a single narrative voice—and its childlike and weak-minded participants.

Besides establishing Stein's maturity and insight through a mother-child trope, her anecdotal method in the *Autobiography* indirectly conveys other aspects of her character that help explain her centrality in the movement toward modernism. For example, Chapter 4, "Gertrude Stein Before She Came to Paris," can be disappointing to a reader expecting an account of how Stein's inner nature was formed by her early experience. Instead, we receive a series of anecdotes that stress, as usual, the piquant and comic in her world and contemporaries, especially during her years at Radcliffe and Johns Hopkins. Nevertheless, through this miscellaneous, digressive, and anecdotal account of the first thirty years of Stein's life there flow several motifs that constitute a self-interpretation of her basic temperament. Here, we discover, is a woman who is slowly but self-consciously learning to pursue her life outside the conventional guidelines for a woman of her class and background. She takes courses principally in psychology and philosophy at Harvard, in itself an unusual program, and then, because it is spring and her evenings have been occupied by the opera, she fails to sit for final examination, explaining that she does not "feel a bit like an examination paper in philosophy today" (79). At Johns Hopkins she does well in her first two years as a medical student but is "bored" by the practical training of her final two years and does not take a degree. We are learning, within anecdotal accounts of the character of William James

and the Hopkins school of medicine, of her unorthodox and independent strength of mind—the quality that not only will take her to Paris
to lead her own life as she wishes but also will underlie her role within
the modernist movement.

Probably the most decisive means by which her anecdotal method
contributes to a favorable appreciation of who and what Gertrude Stein
was in the development of modernism is through her use of anecdotal
reportage to express her basic beliefs about the nature of art and, more
particularly, her own writing. Early in the *Autobiography,* Stein recounts
her relationship to the art dealer Vollard, from whom she and her
brother Leo are attempting to purchase a portrait by Cézanne. Vollard
is an eccentric whose reluctance to assist the Steins in making an
expensive purchase is narrated as a shaggy-dog story. Finally, Stein and
her brother persuade Vollard to show them two portraits, one of a man
and the other of a woman. They decide to purchase the picture of the
woman, and the anecdote concludes:

> Vollard said of course ordinarily a portrait of a woman always is more
> expensive than a portrait of a man but, said he looking at the picture
> more carefully, I suppose that with Cézanne it does not make any dif-
> ference. They put it in a cab and they went home with it. It was this
> picture that Alfy Maurer used to explain was finished and you could tell
> that it was finished because it had a frame.
>
> It was an important purchase because in looking and looking at the
> picture Gertrude Stein wrote Three Lives. (33–34)

The anecdote is typical not only in its witty final remarks—both
Vollard's and Maurer's—but also in Stein's intention to startle the reader,
at the conclusion, into a realization that there is indeed a connection
between the seemingly inconsequential anecdote about Vollard as an
extraordinarily passive dealer in Cézannes and the central thrust of the
work as a whole. The purchase of the Cézanne will contribute to the
cubist form of *Three Lives,* and by inescapable inference, the creation of
Three Lives will chart Stein's course as a champion and exponent of the
new art emerging out of prewar Paris.

In this by no means isolated instance of the introduction of a significant idea about Stein's writing, and thus the history of modern art,
into a seemingly trivial anecdote—as elsewhere—the technique appears to be abrupt and underdeveloped.[11] What *is* the relationship, the

11. In addition to the Matisse anecdote discussed below, see those Stein relates on pp. 156,
211.

Stein's desk in the atelier, with Matisse' *Femme au chapeau* and Picasso's portrait
Yale Collection of American Literature, Beinecke Rare Book and Manuscript Library, Yale University. Used by permission.

reader might well ask, between the Cézanne and *Three Lives?* The question is not answered here or, indeed, in full, anywhere else. Rather, the *Autobiography* accretes—through fragmented comments in the anecdotes—an interpretation of the fundamental assumptions of both modernism in general and Stein's personal aesthetic in particular. For example, soon after the anecdote about Vollard, Stein embarks on a series of anecdotes about the hardships and difficulties of Matisse' early career. The stories conclude with her account of the purchase of Matisse' *Femme au chapeau* at a crucial moment in his career, an anecdote that contains the remark that Matisse was working on his radical painting *Le Bonheur de vivre* at the time of the purchase. Stein then comments, "It was in this picture that Matisse first clearly realized his intention of deforming the drawing of the human body in order to harmonize and intensify the colour values of all the simple colours mixed only with white. He used his distorted drawings as a dissonance is used in music or as vinegar or lemons are used in cooking or egg shells in coffee to clarify. . . . Cézanne had come to his unfinishedness and distortion of necessity, Matisse did it by intention" (41).

This brilliantly compressed and perceptive interpretation of distortion in modern art is followed almost immediately by Stein's remark that just as Matisse was then working on *Le Bonheur de vivre,* she was herself "planning her long book, The Making of Americans, [in which] she was struggling with her sentences, those long sentences that had to be so exactly carried out. Sentences not only words but sentences and always sentences have been Gertrude Stein's life long passion" (41). The extended recounting of Matisse' difficulties thus serves to introduce two briefly stated but cogent observations about modern art and Stein's relation to it. Conscious distortion of traditional visual representation to achieve clarity and emphasis underlies much pictorial modernism, and conscious distortion of conventional narrative representation—that is, a reliance on character and event—to stress the sentence as the center of meaning underlies Stein's analogous efforts in modernist prose.

Each of the major autobiographical works I take up in this study, including Miller's *Tropic of Cancer,* contains a variant of this threefold conjoining of personal narrative (what I did as an expatriate), personal aesthetic (how what I did gave rise to a specific theory and practice of art), and generalized aesthetic (how my own writing is related to modernism). Hemingway's articulation of an expatriate personal and general aesthetic is the least abstract of the four writers', but a set of beliefs about composition and commitment nevertheless emerges clearly out of the contrast between his own values and practice as a writer and those of many of his fellow expatriates. Stein is more conscious than Hemingway of a need to establish her role as interpreter and exemplar of modernism, and therefore she includes considerably more generalized commentary on her efforts and goals as a writer. And Nin and Miller make the quest for a personal aesthetic, an aesthetic that is spelled out frequently and fully, a dominant theme in their works. Yet, despite the differences in the degree of explicitness and the nature of the concept of art announced in each of these autobiographies, all are similar in relating the emergence of a personal aesthetic to the Paris moment.

The three formal devices of the *Autobiography* that I have been discussing—a conjoined narrative voice, an epistemological or cubist narrative structure, and an anecdotal narrative method—pervade the work. Since the *Autobiography* also has a single overarching theme—the celebration of Stein's role (with the aid of Toklas) in establishing modernism—it might be expected that the work succeeds or fails as a whole. Almost all critical commentators on the *Autobiography,* however, have noted a gradual falling-off in literary quality as the work progresses—from the sparkle and depth of implication of the opening portion to the doldrums of the long final chapter. It will help explain this anomaly, as well as shed light on some of Stein's most compelling themes in her depiction of the Paris moment, if a closer than customary look is taken at the distinctive nature of each of the principal sections of the work.

By sections I do not mean the numbered and titled chapters in the book but rather the chief chronological divisions, which are also the chief thematic divisions. The first of these, before Toklas' arrival in Paris in 1907, comprises the first four chapters. The second, from 1907 to 1914, is a single long chapter detailing the full flowering of Stein's role in the new art of prewar France. The last, from 1914 to the "present" of 1932, consists of the final two chapters, which attend to the growth of Stein's fame as well as to the turns in her creative interests.

As I have already noted, the first section of the *Autobiography* is structured around Toklas' process of coming to know Stein. After an opening chapter of only three pages on Toklas' life before arriving in Paris, there is a chapter on her meeting Stein in 1907 and then two more on what she comes to know of Stein's earlier life. The four chapters are additionally built around a number of striking and deeply suggestive symbolic devices: Stein's announcement, early in Chapter 2, of the importance of the year 1907 in the development of modernism and her use at this point and throughout the section of five major creative acts to support this claim, and Stein's dramatic evocation of Paris as a community of like spirits, a community which has indeed provided the matrix for the triumph of the new that the five creative acts represent.

The second chapter, "My Arrival in Paris," opens with the announcement "This was the year 1907. Gertrude Stein was just seeing through the press Three Lives which she was having privately printed, and she was deep in The Making of Americans, her thousand page book. Picasso had just finished his portrait of her . . . which is now so famous, and he had just begun his strange complicated picture of three women. Matisse had just finished his Bonheur de Vivre, his first big composition. . . . It was the moment Max Jacob has since called the heroic age of cubism" (6). As has frequently been remarked, Stein's dating is faulty. George Wickes noted some years ago that "to bring Alice B. Toklas on at a climactic moment, the events of three or four years are concentrated into one." [12] For of the five creative acts of this

12. George Wickes, *Americans in Paris* (Garden City, N.Y., 1969), 53.

"heroic" moment, only two—Picasso's working on *Les Demoiselles d'Avignon* and Stein's being deep in *The Making of Americans*—can be ascribed to the early fall of 1907, when Toklas arrived in Paris and she and Stein met. *Three Lives* was not in press until 1909, Picasso had completed his portrait of Stein in the late summer of 1906, and Matisse had finished his *Bonheur de vivre* that same year.

Wickes is correct in attributing this chronological telescoping to Stein's desire to imply that Toklas' arrival and the start of her relationship with Stein are linked to the triumphant emergence of the new in painting and writing. Here, Stein seems to be saying, are the parallel beginnings of all that has been vital in my life and art. But a concentration on the role of the heroic moment of 1907 in the love story of the *Autobiography* obscures another of Stein's motives in introducing the five events. For once introduced, the events become symbolic motifs in a tapestry of cross-reference to the central theme of the section—the nature of modernism and Stein's role in its origins—despite the section's largely episodic and anecdotal account of Stein's life to 1907. Thus, *Three Lives* is later commented on in connection both with Stein's purchase of the portrait by Cézanne and with Picasso's portrait of her. *The Making of Americans* and Matisse' *Bonheur de vivre* are jointly related to the emergence of a modernist ethos at the close of the portion of Chapter 3 devoted to Matisse. Stein and Toklas visit Picasso's studio, where they examine his strange new work, *Les Demoiselles d'Avignon*. And Picasso's difficulty in completing his portrait of Stein is a major anecdote.

The constant reintroduction of the five events—of which I have mentioned only the leading instances—plays a double role in the first section. It establishes the vital connection between painting and writing in the creation of the new. Stein's own two great breakthroughs into modernism—*Three Lives* and *The Making of Americans*—are yoked in genesis and nature with the work of Picasso and Matisse and are heightened in significance by the association. But the constant reintroduction also, as I have already suggested, imparts a thematic coherence to what would otherwise be a rambling and undirected account of Stein's life to 1907. Stein's claim on our attention as a founder and exemplar of modernism is given validity less by her explicit assertion of it than by her frequent association—in dramatic scene and incidental allusion—of her work and thought with the specific and compelling symbolic equivalents of modernism that the five events represent.

The second symbolic device in the first section—the evocation of

Paris as a matrix for artistic creativity—is particularized in Stein's presentation of 27 rue de Fleurus as the heart of the great experiments in modernism. Immediately after the opening paragraphs of Chapter 2 in which Stein introduces the five momentous creative acts, we are observing Toklas' first Saturday evening at rue de Fleurus. Initially, there is a dinner in the small dining room of the *pavillon,* which is attended by Picasso and Fernande. Later, in the much larger atelier, a number of guests, almost all artists, and including Matisse, arrive. The atelier itself is a symbolic equivalent of Stein's world during the heroic moment. On its walls, from eye level to ceiling, are works by Cézanne, Picasso, Matisse, and other modernists, and in the center of the room is Stein's huge Renaissance writing table, the one in the frontispiece photograph by Man Ray.

The conversation, during the dinner party and in the atelier afterward, is of art, much of it about the new work to be seen the following day at the vernissage (or preview) of the Salon des Indépendants. But the occasion—as is to be true of the entire history of 27 rue de Fleurus in its role as a matrix of the arts—is also very much a social moment. Accompanying the talk are good things to eat and drink—as Hemingway was to recall thirty-five years after his own visits—and the talk is lively and witty as well as perhaps profound. Here too, as Toklas was to note of the vernissage itself (19), is an occasion strikingly different from anything encountered in America: one where men (and not "merely" women) take art seriously. Thus, the entire evening is an almost ritual affirmation and celebration of the community of art, an evening in which food, drink, and conversation mix to produce not only a temporary efflorescence of the spirit but also a powerful and sustaining endorsement of the common effort of those present to re-create the form of artistic expression. Stein, in her strategic placing and full dramatic representation of the moment, is isolating, in the particularity of her dining room and atelier, what was to her the essential meaning of Paris as a center of the arts and of her own growth as an artist: the sense of community possible in the city, a community that exists above all in shared beliefs about the nature and importance of art but that is also affirmed and symbolized by a social moment, by, in short, the coming-together of like minds at 27 rue de Fleurus.

Stein's principal symbol of the nurturing potential of Paris, the atelier, bears comparing with Hemingway's, the café. The two are similar at least insofar as both the atelier and the café are distinctively Parisian social settings and both involve the consumption of food and drink in

an atmosphere of artistic creativity. But there are differences as well, in
that the atelier, as depicted by Stein, is above all a place of communion—a place where she cordially receives her many visitors and engages
them in long conversations, as indeed she was to do with Hemingway—
whereas the café is for Hemingway a place of solitary consumption and
work, like the "good café" or the Closerie de Lilas.[13] Each writer,
including, as we shall see, Nin and Miller, establishes for himself or
herself a symbol of creative freedom and productivity characteristic of
his or her Paris experience. But though the common base of the
symbols is freedom and productivity, each symbol also projects the
specific and distinctive bias of the writer. Stein's atelier, Hemingway's
café, and as a further example, Miller's mean streets constitute both a
collective response to the Paris moment and the capacity of the writer
to express within that response his or her distinctive vision of the process
of creation.

The second section of the *Autobiography*, Chapter 5, "1907–1914,"
opens, "And so life in Paris began and as all roads lead to Paris, all of
us are now there, and I can begin to tell what happened when I was
of it" (86). Life in Paris began, of course, not only in the obvious sense
of the beginning of Toklas' relationship with Stein but also in the sense
established by the first section of the *Autobiography:* that modernism was
now firmly rooted and its full flowering could occur. The image of all
roads leading to Paris, however, requires amplification and qualification,
which Toklas herself undertakes as she shortly afterward comments,
"But to return to the beginning of my life in Paris. It was based upon
the rue de Fleurus and the Saturday evenings and it was like a kaleidoscope slowly turning" (89).

All roads, that is, lead to the atelier at 27 rue de Fleurus as the
symbolic heart of Paris, and the seven years of life there that are to be
depicted have a timeless spatiality. They exist in the memory not as a
precise sequence of events but as an endlessly revolving, and therefore
spatial rather than chronological, body of experience. Stein's world
during this period has a firm and unchanging spatial center—the atelier—and to it come a stream of visitors, mostly painters, whose stories
and personalities and relationships to Stein form a timeless present of
1907–1914, timeless because time has collapsed around place.

13. Susan S. Friedman ("Women's Autobiographical Selves: Theory and Practice," in *The
Private Self: Theory and Practice of Women's Autobiographical Writings,* ed. Shari Benstock [Chapel
Hill, N.C., 1988], 34–62) associates Stein's emphasis on community with a distinctively feminine
search for shared values.

One of the few events narrated at some length which occur outside the kaleidoscope of the rue de Fleurus is the banquet for Rousseau. (This is not dated in the *Autobiography;* it took place in the early fall of 1908.) The paintings of the douanier Rousseau were much ridiculed by conventional art critics for their primitive simplicity and surreal themes. So what better way for his fellow explorers of the new to assert his worth than to offer him a mock banquet in which beneath the farcical joviality of the occasion there lies an effort to assert their common purpose? The banquet, in Picasso's Montmartre studio, was originally planned to be catered. The food fails to arrive, however, and there is much consternation, but Stein and Fernande make some purchases and prepare a large rice dish and all goes forward with much hilarity while a painting by Rousseau, resting on a chair, occupies the place of honor at the head of the table. The incident is therefore not an anomaly in its setting outside rue de Fleurus but rather reinforces the basic theme associated with Saturday evenings at the atelier. For here, too, a group of like-minded artists celebrate, with food and drink, the community of the spirit possible within the Paris moment.

As the second section of the *Autobiography* approaches its conclusion, there are signs of change, indicating the beginning of a reassertion of control by the temporal. For the first time, Americans are among the visitors at the rue de Fleurus, with Carl Van Vechten and John Reed among the earliest. Leo Stein, who has been mentioned from time to time as a resident at 27 rue de Fleurus but otherwise ignored, moves to Florence. And Picasso, the central figure in Stein's relationship to modernism in painting, settles some distance away and becomes a less frequent visitor. Most significant, the war looms, first on the horizon in brief allusions and then, in the summer of 1914, when Stein and Toklas are visiting England, as an immediate presence. The Edenic timelessness of Stein's Paris years from 1907 to 1914, like the timelessness of Hemingway's winters at Schruns before his fall from Eden, ends with a return to history. "The old life was over" (142), Stein notes at the conclusion of the section, in counterpoise to the "And so life in Paris began" of the opening. Our sense is of a fresh and exciting existence—that of the Paris of both a new art arising out of the shared efforts of a community of artists and a rich personal relationship that has its base in freedom—abruptly and definitively interrupted.

The account of Stein's and Toklas' war years, however, in Chapter 6, "The War," the first chapter of the third and last section of the *Autobiography,* is anticlimactic after the anticipation raised by the portentous conclusion of the second section. It is not to be expected that two apolitical, middle-aged women will share the youthful Dos Passos' desire to see the fighting at firsthand or feel his anger at the perversion of American ideals which the war represented. But anyone living through the war years in France might be expected to register some recognition of the physical horrors and personal chaos that the war bore for almost all its participants. Instead, Toklas and Stein at first react to the war mostly as an inconvenient and tedious interruption in their normal pattern of life. There are few visitors to the rue de Fleurus, it is difficult to travel, and the streets of Paris are dark and often deserted. To escape, they spend almost a full year in Mallorca, where they lead a "pleasant" life (165). On returning to Paris in the spring of 1916, they decide to "get into the war" (168). Stein acquires a car, and she and Toklas spend much of 1917 and 1918 dispensing gifts to the wounded in hospitals in the south of France. That incurs many amusing adventures with their automobile and a lengthy "comfortable" stay at Nîmes (180).[14]

The weakness here is in Stein's ingenuous trivialization of the impact of the war on the lives and thought of an entire generation. The first two sections of the *Autobiography* display Stein during a vital moment of transition in belief and perspective, in which she is both an influential participant and a perceptive observer. But whatever entertainment might inhere in her anecdotal account of her war experiences, she is, during this period of cataclysmic change in western belief, both an outsider and seemingly blind.

Our sense of Stein's marginalization in the life of her times continues into the final chapter of the *Autobiography,* Chapter 7, "After the War, 1919–1932." Stein and Toklas return to Paris in early 1919. The "old crowd" is gone but is soon replaced by "new people"; that is, fewer French painters frequent the atelier, but they are replaced by English and American writers. Many of the familiar figures of the expatriate movement are visitors and are briefly characterized: Sylvia Beach, for example, and Sherwood Anderson, T. S. Eliot, Ezra Pound, and (more fully than the others) Ernest Hemingway. And Stein's own work is for the first time being sought by magazines and publishing houses and is receiving critical and public recognition.

---

14. There are two minor exceptions to the blandness of Stein's remarks on the war. She comments very briefly on how "terrifying" the trenches are (187), and she notes, also very briefly, the effect of the war on patriotism and religious belief (227).

Together the continued activity of the atelier and Stein's growing reputation would seem to amount to a triumphant conclusion for the story of a woman who has sought to fashion, within the confines of the rue de Fleurus, both her own way of life and a new literature and art. Cubism and its offshoots are now accepted as the dominant current in art, Stein's own work is gaining fame, and her fellow writers in English are beating a path to her door. But although the central theme of the section is indeed that of triumph, the theme is unconsciously undercut by two pronounced motifs accompanying it, both of which flow from the anecdotes about visitors to the rue de Fleurus.

The first motif concerns the people who are now excluded from the atelier. Throughout the *Autobiography,* visitors to the rue de Fleurus are welcomed, and invited to return, if they are "interesting" or "amusing." In the first two sections, the criterion for this favorable judgment is usually creative vitality, as with Picasso and Matisse, or wit and play of mind, as with Apollinaire. But in the last section the basis of evaluation becomes the degree to which the visitor pays homage to the genius and importance of Gertrude Stein. The change signals the end of the fruitful interaction between Stein and her visitors. Whereas Picasso and Matisse have, before the war, a long and rich association with Stein, Eliot and Pound, after the war, receive short shrift. Neither is deeply or openly appreciative of Stein's significance, and thus both are found unamusing and do not return to the atelier. Hemingway, on the other hand, is initially much engaged by Stein's ideas and writing, which makes him of interest to her despite her recognition of his personal weaknesses. She at first enjoys their long talks, in which he mostly "listened and looked" (212).

But his later apostasy—after the successes of *The Sun Also Rises* and *A Farewell to Arms*—must also be confronted, and thus his portrait turns into an extraordinary exercise in the "putting down" of Hemingway for his gaucheries as writer and man.[15]

If three of the most commanding postwar writers—Eliot, Pound, and Hemingway—lack true discipleship, there are many available to take their place. And in who is now included in the atelier is the second motif undermining the theme of triumph. The figures Stein welcomes as interesting and amusing at 27 rue de Fleurus consist largely of the now-forgotten or the distinctly third-rate: Eliot Paul and Louis Brom-

15. For a vigorous defense of Stein vis-à-vis Hemingway, see Marjorie Perloff, " 'Ninety Percent Rotarian': Gertrude Stein's Hemingway," *American Literature,* LXII (1990), 668–83.

field and Bravig Imbs, for example. Stein's two great personal enthusiasms at the close of the *Autobiography*—artists who are given as much positive attention as the great cubists of an earlier period—are the French writer Bernard Faÿ and the English painter Sir Francis Rose, both of whom are reciprocally enthusiastic about Stein's work.

The weakness of the last section of the *Autobiography*, a section taking up almost a third of the book as a whole, prevents the *Autobiography* from ranking as a completely successful work. But this judgment is not to deny the suggestiveness, liveliness, and structural sophistication of the first two sections. There, in the ingenious and compelling discovery of a form expressive of her love for Toklas and in her discovery as well of modernist techniques expressive of her deepest convictions about both the nature of modern art and the role of Paris in the nurturing of that art, Stein created one of the most distinctive and permanent evocations of the expatriate Paris moment.

The Diary of Anaïs Nin, 1931–1934

The inclusion of *The Diary of Anaïs Nin, 1931–1934* in a study of American expatriate writing between the wars raises several questions. In what sense is Nin an American expatriate writer, given her European background? In what sense is the *Diary*, as a journal, a creative work analogous to the memoirs and novels that are the subject of study elsewhere in this volume?[1] And what is the relationship of the *Diary*, as a revelation of Nin's life in Paris during the early 1930s, to the many other works by her that deal with this period in her life?

Nin's father was Spanish, her mother of Danish and Creole American descent.[2] Nin herself was born in France in 1903 and lived there and

1. Throughout this chapter, I will refer to Nin's 1931–1934 diary in its published form as the *Diary* despite there being many other published volumes of her diary that contain *Diary* in the title.

2. Noël Riley Fitch's *Anaïs: The Erotic Life of Anaïs Nin* (Boston, 1993) is less an interpretative biography than an ill-tempered enumeration of the many discrepancies between the "facts" of Nin's life and their telling in the published diaries. The best introductory account of Nin's background and life therefore remains Gunther Stuhlmann's Introduction to *A Literate Passion: Letters of Anaïs Nin and Henry Miller, 1932–1953* (New York, 1987), v–xxi. Also useful are biographical articles and reminiscences in the journal *Anaïs*.

in Spain until 1914. Nevertheless, despite this background, Nin considered herself American.[3] She lived in New York from 1914 to late 1924, was educated in the New York City schools, married an American, Hugh Guiler, in 1923, and was an American citizen who, after returning to New York at the onset of the Second World War, spent the remainder of her long life in the United States. Most of all, Nin, who was fluent in French, made the conscious decision to write in English. Nin is identified with the expatriate experience not only through her involvement with Henry Miller but also, as we shall see, through her interpretation of her life in Paris during the early 1930s as an escape from a restrictive world to one of freedom and creativity.

The question whether the *Diary* is an imaginative work is related both to how it was edited for publication and to its difference from Nin's other accounts of the period. As an immediately recorded account of daily experiences, thoughts, and feelings, a diary would appear to lack the possibility of the writer's reflective shaping of large-scale themes into expressive form which is characteristic of a novel or memoir. Yet the *Diary* is a "made" work in several respects. In numerous interviews and recollections, Nin and her editor, Gunther Stuhlmann, described the large impact of editing on the published *Diary*.[4] Some material— most notably concerning the existence of her husband, Guiler, and the sexual nature of her relationship to Miller—was cut because she did not wish to offend figures still alive in 1966, when the *Diary* was prepared for publication. Furthermore, a good many entries were omitted or severely cut because they were repetitious or, in Nin's estimation, poorly written. But most important of all, both Nin and Stuhlmann had a clear sense, some thirty years after the recorded events of the early 1930s, of the nature and role of this moment in Nin's development. With a theme in mind, she and Stuhlmann consciously structured the *Diary,* both by the selection of material and by its organization into sections, to express the theme.[5] Nothing was added, Nin insisted, and

3. See especially Nin's comments in Krishna Baldev Vaid's "Writing and Wandering: A Talk with Anaïs Nin," *Anaïs,* V (1987), 49–55.

4. See Anaïs Nin, "Genesis of the Diary," in *The Novel of the Future* (Athens, Ohio, 1970); Duane Schneider, *An Interview with Anaïs Nin* (Athens, Ohio, 1970); Evelyn J. Hinz, ed., *A Woman Speaks: The Lectures, Seminars, and Interviews of Anaïs Nin* (Chicago, 1975); Benjamin Franklin V and Duane Schneider, *Anaïs Nin: An Introduction* (Athens, Ohio, 1979), 167–76; and Vaid, "Writing and Wandering."

5. See Gunther Stuhlmann's Introduction to *The Diary of Anaïs Nin, 1931–1934* (New York, 1966), v–xii. There, in noting that he and Nin selected only half the available diary material for publication, he also announces an explicit theme for the *Diary.*

very little was rewritten, but much was omitted—from 50 to 90 percent, according to different accounts—with the entire process conducted, Nin remarked, in the spirit of the novelist.[6]

The character of the *Diary* as a distinctive work of art can also be validated by comparing it with Nin's other writings about this phase of her life. A sizable portion of the material omitted from the period covered by the *Diary* has recently been published in two volumes, as *Henry and June: From the Unexpurgated Diary of Anaïs Nin* (1986) and *Incest: From a Journal of Love—The Unexpurgated Diary of Anaïs Nin, 1932–1934* (1992). In these selections from her diaries, Nin and her editors project a more sensual and emotionally disturbed figure than that of the *Diary*. In 1987, there also appeared *A Literate Passion: Letters of Anaïs Nin and Henry Miller, 1932–1953,* which displays her as far more engaged in the practical matters of existence than do the diaries. And, finally, the fiction Nin wrote between 1931 and 1934—*The House of Incest* and *The Winter of Artifice*—depict Nin's deep involvement with her father, Joaquin Nin, and with June Miller (two figures who also play significant roles in the *Diary*), in the mode of the symbolic prose poem, a mode very distant from the analytical and often wry style of the *Diary*.[7] In brief, Nin initially gave her diary entries a distinctive expressive coloration different from that of her other accounts of this period, and she later shaped the entries into a distinctive vision of her life. Nin's *Diary* is a fully conscious and formed work of art.

The *Diary* opens with Nin attempting to find a publisher for her just-completed *D. H. Lawrence: An Unprofessional Study*.[8] That Lawrence' ideas had come as a revelation to Nin is suggested by her unqualified praise of them in her study and her frequent citation of his insights in

6. Nin, *The Novel of the Future,* 153–54; Hinz, ed., *A Woman Speaks,* 151. Stuhlmann (*Diary,* xi) states that half the material was omitted; Nin, in 1967, recalled that she included only 10 percent of the diary in the published version (Schneider, *An Interview with Anaïs Nin,* 5). The original diaries have been preserved, but their relationship to the published versions has not as yet been fully studied.

7. The *Diary* makes clear that these works, though published in 1936 and 1939, were written for the most part during 1933 and 1934.

8. Despite the great interest of recent years in Nin's life and work, there have been remarkably few studies of the *Diary* as a literary work. But for some useful commentary, see Lynn Z. Bloom and Orlee Holder, "Anaïs Nin's *Diary* in Context," in *Women's Autobiography: Essays in Criticism,* ed. Estelle C. Jelinek (Bloomington, Ind., 1980); Duane Schneider, "Anaïs Nin in the *Diary:* The Creation and Development of a Persona," *Mosaic,* XI (1978), 9–19; and Tristine Rainer, "Anaïs Nin's *Diary I:* The Birth of the Young Woman as an Artist," in *A Casebook on Anaïs Nin,* ed. Robert Zaller (New York, 1974), 161–68.

the *Diary* itself. A Lawrencian theme which especially attracted Nin was his belief in experience as motion. Life to Lawrence, Nin wrote in her study, "is a process of *becoming,* a combination of states we have to go through. Where people fail is that they wish to elect a state and remain in it. This is a kind of death."[9] Although, as we shall see, Nin often expresses the need for personal mobility by means of spatial metaphors similar to Hemingway's, she relies principally on the device of encasing new ideas, new experiences, and new feelings in specific individuals. Nin's escape from a death-in-life stasis is achieved by iden- tifying fresh possibilities of life for herself in the lives of others. What- ever the obscure comprehension and ambivalent response that Nin brought to specific personal relationships during the actual Paris mo- ment of 1931–1934, she in the *Diary* crafts those relationships into a meaningful explanation of what she believes she has become by the conclusion of the period.

Many figures are named and discussed in the *Diary,* including a number of secondary characters of considerable interest and importance, such as Fred Perlès, Miller's close friend; William Bradley, a perceptive and sympathetic publisher; and Hilaire Hiler, Nin's fellow student of psychoanalysis. But plainly the *Diary* centers on six primary characters: Henry Miller, June Miller, René Allendy, Antonin Artaud, Joaquin Nin, and Otto Rank. These are the chief figures in Nin's life, whether judged by the attention they receive in the *Diary* or the role each plays in Nin's "process of *becoming*." The six fall into a number of striking patterns in relation to one another and to Nin, patterns that constitute the themes and form of the *Diary.*

In the *Diary's* chronological ordering, the six fall into two sequential groups or tiers of meaning for Nin. The three figures who deeply engage her from late 1931, when the *Diary* opens, to early 1933 are Henry Miller, his wife, June, and the psychoanalyst René Allendy. But June Miller leaves Paris for a second and final time, Allendy's influence wanes, and Henry Miller—though continuing to play a major role in Nin's life—is no longer a fresh source of self-identification. Hence, in early 1933 her attention turns to the actor and writer Antonin Artaud, to her father, Joaquin Nin, and to the psychoanalyst Otto Rank.

Several major threads of connectedness exist between the two tiers of relationships and among the figures in each tier. Each group contains a powerful father figure (Henry Miller or Joaquin Nin), an attractive

9. Anaïs Nin, *D. H. Lawrence: An Unprofessional Study* (1932; rpr. Denver, 1964), 20.

but destructive and self-destructive passionate temperament (June Miller or Artaud), and a wise counselor (Allendy or Rank). Each tier is also organized around a set of interior triangles that provide the psychic intensity that, in conjunction with the tensions present in individual relationships, is the fuel, or the emotional energy, necessary for Nin's intellectual and psychological mobility and growth. Each of Nin's relationships—from that with Miller initially to that with Rank at the close—is told as a love story in which Nin is at first deeply absorbed in her partner, then gradually disillusioned, and finally dismissive. And, as in most love stories, the specific relationship is in competition with other personal commitments. Thus the first tier of relationships includes two triangles: Nin is engaged simultaneously by Henry and June Miller, and Henry Miller and Allendy compete for Nin. And in the second tier, Artaud and Joaquin Nin compete for Nin's allegiance and love. In addition, the two tiers are not only symetrically structured and balanced but also, as a result of the learning process that they provide for Nin, constitute a progressive movement. Destructive or false guides (June Miller, Artaud, and Joaquin Nin) and those who have lost their potency (Allendy) are discarded, and there remain only Henry Miller and, above all, in a kind of triumphant conclusion, Otto Rank, in his role as validator of the becoming that has occupied Nin for the previous three years.

Although Nin confines most of her specific comments about Paris as the scene of her becoming to the passages about her relationship with Henry Miller, the six figures constitute as a whole a metaphor for several important aspects of the Paris expatriate moment. When we first encounter Nin, she is, as in the opening of a perverse fairy tale, a beautiful princess imprisoned not in an ugly castle but in her lovely old house in the quiet and past-bound Paris suburb of Louveciennes. The world outside this "beautiful prison," the world of discovery and change, not only is physically that of Paris—from Miller to Rank, each of the six figures except June lives and works in Paris—but also symbolically reflects the expatriate myth of Paris as a center of freedom and creativity.[10] Henry Miller is the free artist incarnate—unbound from convention both in his life and writing—and June Miller and Artaud live out an even more extreme form of the free expression of self. Allendy and Rank, as analysts, are committed to freeing the individual from subservience to his or her past. Only Joaquin Nin, in his social rigidities and

10. *Diary*, 7. Further citations of this edition will appear in the text.

his determination to return Nin to playing the obedient daughter, stands in opposition to freedom. Collectively, the figures therefore represent for Nin the opportunity for freedom symbolized by her journey on the little train from Louveciennes to Paris—an opportunity to escape the restrictions her past and present life places upon her and to discover ways to live more fully and creatively and thus to begin the process of becoming.

Becoming is therefore not a vague concept in Nin's *Diary*. To become, one must first be free of the physical, social, and psychological limitations placed on belief and feeling by one's past and present circumstances—circumstances that for Nin are defined precisely by the symbolic import of Louveciennes and her father. But escape is also escape to something, and Nin's goal is to establish for herself an awareness and use of her nature as a woman and as an artist. In discovering herself as a woman, she will come to realize both what is distinctive in the feminine temperament and what she may advantageously appropriate from the masculine. She will recognize the need for an androgynous flexibility. As an artist, she will come to realize the powerful and unique insights available to her as a woman artist and will accordingly forge a feminist aesthetic credo. And all of her growth and development, with its accompanying pain and anguish and its frequent indecision yet ultimate triumph, will occur in the context not only of Paris as a physical entity but also of the Paris of the spirit represented by the six figures who will help Nin chart her journey of the self.

The *Diary* opens with images of Nin's home and the village of Louveciennes which are emblematic of her life to this point. The village is a charming backwater, distant both in space and time from the currents of modern life. "On clear nights one can see Paris" (3), but Nin's house is two hundred years old, Louveciennes is a place of relics of the past, and old women sit behind windows and watch the passersby. The life she has been leading is not ugly or distressing; the town and her house have a gracious calm and beauty. But Nin herself is unhappy, for she wishes to live life for its "high moments" (5). The barriers to that, she realizes, are not the house or village. These are merely symbols; the obstacles to an escape into the present and into movement lie "always within one's self" (4). She must overcome such obstacles, however, since she has decided, "I want to be a writer who reminds others that these moments exist; I want to prove that there is infinite space, infinite meaning, infinite dimension" (5).

The house at Louveciennes

In the opening of the *Diary,* Nin lays out several of the basic themes of the work, acquainting us at the same time with her symbolic idiom. She announces a vocation: she will be a writer who functions within the realm of intense and deep emotion. But she is at present blocked from encountering, and hence from doing artistic justice to, this range of experience. She at first renders the obstacles spatially and temporally: Paris is in the distance and her village is enveloped in its past. This physicality, however, is symbolic of the more obdurate barriers within herself: her psychological and emotional distance from the intensities of life that Paris signifies, and her imprisonment in her own past. The turning of the conflict inward, where barriers are amorphous states of mind and feeling rather than clearly defined physical conditions, does not cause her dismay. For inward spatiality is infinite in the sense of richly varied and unending. Once begun, the journey into the Paris of the present will become a permanently rewarding quest for the understanding and expression of the multiplicity of identities that make up Anaïs Nin. "What interests me," Nin will note later in the *Diary,* "is not the core but the potentialities of this core to multiply and expand infinitely. The diffusion of the core, its suppleness and elasticity, rebound, ramifications. Spanning, encompassing, space-devouring, star-trodden journeys, everything around and between the core" (201).

The notion of an inward planetary system awaiting exploration and—in the sense of productive use by the artist—colonization is, however, intimately and paradoxically linked to concrete physicality. The train from Louveciennes to Paris must be taken for the process to begin in earnest, and the Paris of selfhood is a "real" Paris of specific quartiers, cafés, restaurants, and above all individuals. The physical may only symbolize the inward, but the physical is also the indispensable means for discovering the inward self. And for Nin, in her first major evocation in the *Diary* of a world outside Louveciennes and in much of the remainder of the work, the physical is Henry Miller. "The hero of this book," Nin writes, "may be the soul, but it is an odyssey from the inner to the outer world, and it is Henry who is dispelling the fogs of shyness, of solitude, taking me through the street, and keeping me in a café—until dawn" (107).

On several occasions, Nin enlarges on Miller as a guide to seeing and understanding what Paris street life reveals. "We are walking to the Place Clichy," a typical passage begins. "Henry makes me aware of the street, of people. He is smelling the street, observing. He shows me the whore with the wooden stump who stands near the Gaumont

Palace. He shows me the narrow streets winding up, lined with small hotels, and the whores standing by the doorways, under red lights. We sit in several cafés . . . where the pimps are playing cards and watching their women on sidewalks" (77–78). Later Nin writes, "When I walk about Paris, I see and sense much more than I did before, my eyes have been opened by Henry's revelations" (85). What she sees in the streets is above all a reflection of Henry Miller himself—his energy, his vibrancy, his delight in the bizarre physical insistence of life, and his huge and catholic appetite for experience. An intellectual occupied with the thought of his time, Miller is nevertheless committed to the instinctual life—to live, and also to write, at the deepest and most inchoate level of his nature. The streets, therefore, as a metaphor of Miller's vision of himself—and also, as the passage suggests, of the sexual character of his absorption in the primitive self—come as a powerful new force in Nin's life. Miller, she writes, "exposes the withdrawn Anaïs who lives several fathoms deep. He likes to churn the ground. His role is to keep everything moving, for out of chaos comes richness, out of upheaval new seeds" (69).

Miller, in brief, is the principle of "flow" in life, as he himself was to characterize his nature in *Tropic of Cancer*. His ethos is that of moving through, observing, and participating in the streets of experience and thus stimulating a productive churning-up of the ground—the ground in the sense both of an immediately heightened inner life and of an eventual fertile soil for the imagination. As Nin comes to realize, "Henry's daily and continuous flow of life, his sexual activity, his talks with everybody, his café life, his conversations with people in the street, which I once considered an interruption to writing, I now believe to be a quality which distinguishes him from other writers. He never writes in cold blood; he is always writing in white heat" (155). The imagery here, and in similar evocations of Miller's nature and example, is of a powerful masculine strength and sexuality. Nin, in her need to escape from the quiescence of Louveciennes, gratefully absorbs this quality so different from the life of her beautiful prison. She writes, "[Miller] arouses tremendous strength in me. . . . I am conscious of his life. I feel rich with it. His letters and his notes on the back of them, his wealth of activity, give me a feeling of warmth and fervor which I love, a feeling of expansion, of ampleness, plentitude. . . . I no longer have the feeling of emptiness around me" (50). This is a richly suggestive statement of Miller's effect on Nin. He arouses in her her own capacity for strength, for activity, for warmth and fervor, and she feels complete and fulfilled in this expansion of herself. She touches on but does not name outright the two complementary effects of her relationship with Miller: she finds herself sexually fulfilled as a woman, but in this fulfillment there is also a development of masculine attributes. Her sense of "ampleness" and "plentitude" derives partly from an internalization of Miller's "tremendous strength."

Nin thus introduces one of the central themes of the *Diary* through her relationship with Miller: the idea that her growth into mobility and multiplicity springs in large measure from developing the two hitherto reclusive and underemployed halves of her nature, her femininity and her masculinity. The theme of Nin's distinctive nature as a woman will be brought out more fully through her relationship with June Miller, but the side of her temperament that holds the potential for a rich androgynous complementarity is unlocked through her relationship with Henry Miller. Strength and physical vitality such as Miller exhibits are not in opposition to her own fragility and shyness, she comes to understand, but are rather qualities it is necessary for her to recognize as inherent and productive in her own nature. She will later observe, in an image of androgynous harmony, "Talking with Henry I experience the sensation that there will come a time when we will both understand everything, because our masculine and feminine minds are trying to meet, not to fight each other" (184).

Nin's relationship with June Miller is set down in the *Diary* as high drama—even melodrama. Even before arriving in Paris in late 1931, June is vividly actualized in Henry's tortured combination of fear of and desire for her. Then, from her dramatic arrival at Louveciennes—at night, framed in the light of the doorway—she dominates Nin's thoughts and feelings not only for the two months of her stay in Paris but for the remainder of the year. Their relationship is like a tempestuous, brief, and intense love affair. Nin is immediately drawn by June's voluptuous beauty and air of mystery and seeks her out at times when Henry is absent. Nin offers gifts. There is increasing physical intimacy: Nin's touching June's breast and their walking arm in arm, dancing together in a nightclub, and kissing in a cab. Finally, there is a painful separation.

Throughout this love story, Nin paradoxically plays the masculine role of pursuer—paradoxically because she is presumably the more feminine of the two in her timidity and smaller physical frame. In assuming the masculine role—in arranging meetings with June, in pressing gifts upon her, and in being attracted physically by June's sexuality—Nin dramatizes the deep appeal of June's feminine nature. June personifies a feminine potential that Nin has not achieved in her life, that of a capacity to live fully in a dream world, to live a fantasy life where all is beauty and satisfaction. Henry's life, Nin realizes early in her infatuation with June, is one of "earthy, lusty harsh facts. [June] has thrown me back into visions, dreams. But if I were made for reality, for ordinary experience, I would not have loved her. I have a greater need of illusion and dreams, then, than I have of Henry's animal world" (33).

June's capacity to believe in and act out her fantasies lends her an aura of the inscrutable and an apparent depth, since her dream vision of herself—of who and what she is—constantly changes. To Nin, at the height of her susceptibility to June, this capacity is deeply attractive because of its affinity with her own desire for multiplicity of selfhood, for a fluidity of response to the changing circumstances of life. She can declare to June that she is the "only woman who ever answered the fantasies I had about what a woman should be" (24). She amplifies this shortly afterward, in a passage where she attributes to June her own desire for a life without borders: "June's character seems to have no definable form, no boundaries, no core. . . . Do I feel my own self definite, encompassable? I know its boundary lines. There are experiences I shy away from. But my curiosity, creativeness, urge me beyond these boundaries, to transcend my character. My imagination pushes me into unknown, unexplored, dangerous realms. . . . I do not like to be just one Anaïs, whole, familiar, contained. As soon as someone defines me, I do as June does: I seek escape from the confinements of definition" (29).

From their first encounter at Louveciennes, however, when Nin wishes to declare to June, "You are the woman I want to be" (21), Nin has also recognized the other side of June's life of illusion and fantasy, her "enormous ego, false, weak, posturing" (20). June, she sees more and more clearly, uses her beauty, sensuality, and indefinability to gain manipulative power. Among those at risk from the destruction June can cause by wielding her power are not only anonymous steamship clerks (in a long incident narrated by Nin) but Henry and Nin herself. June is disruptive both in Henry's life and in his work, and she is on the edge of becoming so for Nin. Thus, as June's departure approaches, Nin begins to "awaken from [her] dream" and to perceive that June's way of life, if pursued fully, is a kind of hell, a "descent into the irrational level of existence, where the instincts and blind emotions are loose, where one lives by pure impulse, pure fantasy, and therefore pure madness" (36).

With June's departure comes insight into her meaning for Nin which goes beyond a rejection of the "madness" she exemplifies. "I stand between June and Henry," Nin writes, "between his primitive strength . . . and June's illusions and delusions. I am grateful for Henry's abundance and flow. I want to answer him with equal abundance and flow. But I find myself keeping certain secrets, as June did" (47). Nin's immersion in the turmoil of the lives of Henry and June has given her not only an awareness of her androgynous multiplicity but also the conviction that this aspect of her nature must extend into the most intimate area of experience, the sexual. "The love of only one man or one woman is a limitation," she declares. "To be fully alive is to live unconsciously and instinctively in all directions, as Henry and June do. Idealism is the death of the body and of the imagination. All but freedom, utter freedom, is death" (42).

The tension between a desire to absorb June's passionate femininity and a realization of the dangers this entails continues throughout 1932 as Nin and Miller frequently discuss the meaning of June while they seek to re-create her in their writing. The tension comes to a head in late 1932 with June's dramatic reappearance in Paris. Nin again finds herself drawn to June but is now even more strongly repelled by her destructiveness. June's proximity to madness comes out fully in an ugly scene in which she and Henry become drunk and sick and violent. Nin wishes to escape from the sordidness of June as well as from the triangle she finds herself enmeshed in—a desire fulfilled by June's second and final departure. But even with June gone, Nin, in later reexpressing her wish "to live only for ecstasy," still does so by the metaphor June's nature supplies: "I am aware also that I am becoming June" (174).

Nin encapsulates the impact of her acceptance of an androgynous self and the implications of the acceptance for her sexuality in a brief but highly charged scene that occurs shortly after June's first departure, when she and Miller visit a whorehouse. There is a somewhat different presentation of the same incident in *Henry and June,* where the themes inherent in the version in the *Diary* are even more explicit.

In the *Diary*'s description of the incident, Miller suggests that he and Nin visit a whorehouse and he selects an establishment at 32 rue Blondel. There they are entertained by two whores. One, a dark woman, plays the masculine role, the other—younger, smaller, and blond—the feminine. All is at the level of bantering both for the whores and for Miller and Nin

> until . . . The small woman had been lying on her back with her legs open. The big woman removed the penis and kissed the small woman's clitoris. She flicked her tongue over it, caressed it, kissed. The small woman's eyes closed and we could see she was enjoying it. She began to moan and tremble with pleasure. She offered to our eyes her quivering body and raised herself a little to meet the voracious mouth of the bigger woman. And then came the climax for her and she let out a cry of joy. Then she lay absolutely still. Breathing fast. A moment later they both stood up, joking, and the mood passed. (60)

In *Henry and June,* it is Hugh Guiler and Anaïs who visit the whorehouse on the rue Blondel, and at Nin's suggestion. Again Nin and her companion observe the prostitutes:

> Hugo and I look on, laughing a little at their sallies. We learn nothing new. It is all unreal, until I ask for the lesbian poses.
> The little woman loves it, loves it better than the man's approach. The big woman reveals to me a secret place in the woman's body, a source of a new joy, which I had sometime sensed but never definitely— that small core at the opening of the woman's lips, just what the man passes by. There, the big woman works with the flicking of her tongue. The little woman closes her eyes, moans, and trembles in ecstasy. Hugo and I lean over them, taken by that moment of loveliness in the little woman, who offers to our eyes her conquered, quivering body. Hugo is in turmoil. I am no longer woman; I am man. I am touching the core of June's being. . . .
> And when we returned home, he adored my body because it was lovelier than what he had seen and we sank into sensuality together with new realization. We are killing phantoms.[11]

It will be recalled that because Hugh Guiler—usually called Hugo by Nin—was alive in 1966, she deleted any reference to him from the *Diary.* But that she could in good conscience replace Guiler with Miller in the *Diary* and that she had in her original account tied her sexual excitement to June reveals the essential truth present in both tellings of

11. Rupert Pole, ed., *Henry and June: From the Unexpurgated Diary of Anaïs Nin* (New York, 1986), 71–72.

the event—a truth that draws as well upon the fact that it was Nin who proposed the visit to the whorehouse. What is captured here is the possibility of a sexual awakening independent of a particular partner or agent in the awakening—a sexual awakening, in other words, in which the emphasis is on the meaning of the occasion for selfhood rather than for a specific personal relationship. The large whore is male and female interchangeably, but in the end she is primarily an activating instrument—a tongue—in the fulfillment of a pleasure that is confined to the clitoris of the smaller whore. And so for Nin, for whom the scene comes at a crucial juncture in the movement of self-discovery, there is a dawning—first felt and later fully understood—that Henry, Hugh, and June are in a sense interchangeable agents in bringing her to full self-awareness and that her self-awareness contains both male and female identities. The significance of her recent experience—a significance she sees mirrored in the visit to the whorehouse—is that it is she who has been brought to life and who has, through the discovery of the intensity of her sensual nature, entered deeply into the process of self-identification and thus ultimately of self-expression.[12]

No wonder, then, that Nin during this scene makes love to June in her imagination and that she and Guiler make love that night and that she and Miller have made love for the first time a few days earlier. Nin's point is not to celebrate a female Don Juanism, a libertine sexuality in which sex is an aim in itself, but to announce a sexuality so powerfully oriented toward self-discovery that it reaches, in its final joining of body and soul, a kind of epiphany. Shortly after the scene in the whorehouse, Nin writes, in *Henry and June,* of her lovemaking with Miller: "That last afternoon in Henry's hotel room was for me like a white-hot furnace. Before, I had only white heat of the mind and of the imagination; but now it is of the blood. Sacred completeness."[13]

Nin's "sacred completeness" is both similar to and different from the union of creative energy and sexual expression that is central in the memoirs of Hemingway and Stein and also in Miller's *Tropic of Cancer.* There is in all these writers a discovery in Paris of a sexuality that is also a liberation of the imagination. But for Nin, this discovery is so profoundly solipsistic that it results in the creation of something new. For in Nin's *Diary,* the discovery of sex is also a liberation from the

---

12. It should be noted that a similar stress on Nin rather than on her sexual partner occurs in the anonymity of the father of her stillborn child. See 68n16.

13. Pole, ed., *Henry and June,* 77.

bonds of sexuality so far as the fulfillment of a sexual need implied—
as it did for Hemingway, Stein, and Miller—the acceptance of a body
of traditional belief. For Nin, experience is now a blank page to be
written on by the capacity to feel. This may also have been Miller's
creed. But for Nin, far less intellectual baggage accompanied the idea,
and there was also for her a far greater acceptance of the autocracy of
the feeling self.

The third "romance" Nin portrays during the period of her full
involvement with Henry and June, from late 1931 to late 1932, is
between her and the French psychoanalyst René Allendy. By the time
Nin first approaches Allendy, in the spring of 1932, she has experienced
the liberating effect of penetrating to her own deepest feelings as a
result of her connections with Henry and June. But there remains an
additional self-imposed prison to escape besides that symbolized by
Louveciennes—the one existing in her innermost nature as a result of
her childhood relationship to her father. In an initially painful but
increasingly exhilarating series of analytical sessions with Allendy, Nin
uncovers the emotional deposit left by her father's desertion of his family
when she was twelve—especially her sense that her unworthiness was
the cause of his departure and that she must therefore, in her relationships with men, demonstrate her worth by playing the roles expected
of her.

Allendy, in a kind of wooing, gains Nin's confidence through his
insight and his willingness not to be judgmental. In a scene similar in
its sexual cargo to that of the visit to the whorehouse, Nin confesses
to Allendy her low confidence in her physical attractiveness, especially
in the size of her breasts. He tries to reassure her, and as a test of his
understanding and sympathy she bares her breasts, which Allendy admires. As Nin later admits, her act contains an element of sexual prov-
ocation, of flirting pure and simple. But it is also consistent with her
response to the two whores, in that it betrays an effort to break the
molds of attitude and behavior imposed upon her by the insecurities
of her earlier psychic life. She can meet her fear of inadequacy not by
succumbing to a role demanded by her fear—here maidenly timidity—
but by challenging it and triumphing over it.

Nin's belief that, with Allendy's help, she has broken free of the past
is expressed through one of the most compelling recurrent images of
the *Diary,* that of herself as a mirror reflecting the needs, desires, and
expectations of others. She announces in May, after a number of intense
sessions with Allendy, that she has been engaged in an experiment in

the "laboratory of the soul" and has discovered "that destiny can be directed, that one does not need to remain in bondage to the first wax imprint made on childhood sensibilities. One need not be branded by the first pattern. Once the deforming mirror is smashed, there is a possibility of wholeness; there is a possibility of joy" (105). Nin's triumphant endorsement of the liberating possibilities of psychoanalysis is the fullest and most overt statement by any of the expatriates of the inherent similarity between the goals of expatriation and analysis.[14] Or in her case, between an escape from Louveciennes—which she once described as similar to an American suburb[15]—to Paris and an escape from bondage to the past into a liberated present. One is a spatial, the other a temporal movement, but whether the escape is from a restrictive social environment or a personal history, the emphasis is on the possibility of self-discovery in freedom, and therefore on the possibility of "wholeness" and "joy."

As yet another love story, however, Nin's involvement with Allendy has the same internal rhythm as that of her other major relationships in the *Diary*. She is initially absorbed in the new ways of thinking Allendy represents, and she brings a totality and intensity of preoccupation to the relationship. (Most of the long sections of April and May, 1932, are devoted to her meetings with him.) But gradually, as she draws from the relationship its productive role in her self-definition, it begins both to pale in fervor and to reveal the defects of her "lover." Allendy displays a personal interest in her and appears poised to take advantage of the transference inherent in analysis. He becomes possessive and evinces jealousy of Miller by severely criticizing him. But even worse, he wishes to substitute for Nin's earlier imprisoning self-conception of inadequacy his own limiting and confining conception of her as "charming, feminine, and soft" (118), that is, as conventionally feminine. He will help her break the mirror of selfhood she acquired from her father but will replace it with one reflecting his own expectations for her. Allendy's notion of her as essentially a "good woman" does not take into account Nin's nature and self-expression as an artist seeking intensity and range—the illimitable—in experience. So gradually, as 1932 goes forward, she withdraws from the relationship while still—as was true of

14. An even fuller endorsement occurs at the close of Nin's long account of Otto Rank's beliefs (297–300).

15. "I once found myself, like many young women in their twenties, trapped in a suburban life, and a suburb of Paris is no different than a suburb of New York or Chicago" (Hinz, ed., *A Woman Speaks*, 224–25).

her involvement with Henry and June—retaining as functioning conditions within herself the insights into self-definition and freedom which Allendy had helped her discover.

By early 1933, the first triad of the major relationships Nin depicts in the *Diary* has had its greatest impact and the figures involved are diminishing in importance for her. June leaves Paris for the second and final time in December, 1932. Allendy is no longer central in Nin's thoughts, and Miller, though still significantly present in Nin's life, is no longer a fresh defining force. Enter at this point, then, a second group of three figures: Antonin Artaud; Nin's father, Joaquin Nin; and Otto Rank. The relationships in this second tier are, as I stated earlier, similar to those in the first in a number of ways—not least in that each relationship is also a form of love story and that there are obvious parallels between June Miller and Artaud and between Allendy and Rank. Yet in the aggregate, the figures of the second tier play a different role in Nin's growth as a woman and an artist. Henry Miller, June Miller, and Allendy helped her escape and define herself. Artaud and her father test her ability to stand firm in what she has achieved from the earlier relationships, and Rank validates and lets her extend still farther her acts of liberation and self-definition. The *Diary* as a whole— and not just Nin's sessions with Allendy—therefore has an underlying configuration that squares with the idea of the interior life as a laboratory. Something is learned in a series of interrelated experiments; that knowledge is then tested, is found worthy, and is triumphantly restated.

Like June, Artaud attempts to live life as a form of theater, of illusion creating, and like June, he uses drugs to aid him in this. Artaud finds experience to be mainly pain and anguish, and his life both as man and as writer is devoted to an expression of this truth, as when he acts out a man dying of the black death as the major component of his lecture "The Theatre and the Plague." The qualities in Artaud that attract Nin are much the same as those that attracted her to June: the intensity and purity of his vision of life, and his responsiveness to her own nature. With Artaud, as with June, she is attracted by someone willing to act out his self-conception vibrantly and at all costs. But now, having been "trained" by her experience with June, she is from the first also wary of being absorbed into Artaud's self-vision. She is capable of recognizing the death wish implicit in Artaud's temperament and beliefs—"To be kissed by Artaud was to be drawn toward death, toward insanity" (229)—and therefore, in contrast to her reaction to June, she resists rather than desires a physical consummation. He, however, becomes demanding, and so, in a pattern now fully established, Nin withdraws and regroups.

If Artaud marks a recurrence of Nin's susceptibility to the power of the self-possessed temperament, Joaquin Nin embodies a reemergence of the strong hold of the idea of the father upon her emotions. Joaquin Nin has been present in the *Diary* from its opening pages in Nin's musings on the woman into which he has made her. But now, in early 1933, he appears in more than memory, first through the mediation of a "beautiful letter" (201) in which he seeks to renew their association, and then in person. In the beginning, Nin resists his overtures. She does not need him anymore, she feels. But eventually she agrees to meet, recognizing that she is still held by him, since he was her "first love." The image introduced at this point of a courtship renewed, of a rewooing, becomes the controlling metaphor in the account of their encounters up to the fall of 1933. Nin, at their first meeting, realizes her father's overwhelming egotism and his essential falseness but is also drawn not only by his "gusto for life" (213) but by his effort to please and charm her and his delight in her. She feels vindicated and fulfilled by his pride in her and, as at the height of a courtship, is willing to overlook his faults in the exultation of a relationship confirmed and consummated.

Nin's return, in a sense, to her preadolescent absorption in her father and in his judgment of her reaches its apogee in a holiday she and Joaquin Nin spend in the south of France that is in effect a honeymoon. But soon afterward, as the emotional high of the moment wears off, Nin begins to understand what has happened. To her father, she realizes, she is another prey in his lifelong pursuit of the adoration of women and, now that she has been captured, a tame and obedient ornament, as daughter, to his role as father-conquerer. Artaud wished to absorb her into his sphere of violence and pain, and Joaquin Nin into his paternalistic Don Juanism. Both, that is, wish her to reflect back to her admirers the quality they desire to find in her. But Nin, seared by her experience with June and instructed by Allendy, is now in a position to resist enticements to be a "fairy godmother" (247) to the needs of others projected onto her. And so she gradually disentangles herself from her father's control and world, as she has done from Artaud's.

Nin's initial meeting with the Vienna-born psychoanalyst Otto Rank occurs in November, 1933, when she has broken completely with Artaud and is becoming increasingly disillusioned with her father. Nin had earlier read and admired Rank's *Art and Artist* but had not sought him out. Now, though, having largely dismissed Allendy but troubled by the number and instability of her relationships, she arranges a meeting. There then follows, in imitative form of her intense response to Rank's ideas and person, a long section of the *Diary*—November, 1933–February, 1934—which is completely devoted to his beliefs and to Nin's sessions with him.

Unlike Allendy, Rank treats Nin with no expectation that her state of mind can be easily placed within Freudian categories of analysis: "Rank waits, free, ready to leap, but not holding a trap door in readiness which will click at the cliché phrase. He awaits free. You are a new human being. Unique. He detours the obvious, and begins a vast expansion into the greater, the vaster, the beyond" (289). Rank thus begins his analysis of Nin with an evocative endorsement of the conception of the self as an illimitable space, which has been the principal motif in Nin's sense of her interior journeying and has provided the recurrent spatializing metaphor for the inner self from the earliest pages of the *Diary*. "In digging deeper," Nin remarks of Rank's method, "the universe of our character has become greatly enlarged, unlimited in space" (291).

Rank's belief in the uniqueness and infinitude of the self underlies his explanation and defense of the distance Nin has come in her journey. He explains her multiplicity of selves and thus her need to seek out others to help define various portions of her nature, as well as her androgyny and her discovery that the wellspring of her artistic themes and forms is her feminine temperament. Because Nin has throughout the *Diary* been seeking both a clearer understanding of the distinctiveness of the feminine character and an application of that understanding to herself as an artist, Rank's appeal and meaning for her reside less in new insights than in his articulate confirmation of her deepest feelings about herself. Nin's initial reflections on the special nature of the feminine were tame and conventional: men can live alone in the world, but women live largely through men (106), and women have a special capacity for nurturing (116). Her traditional opinions also included the belief that women lack the masculine capacity for abstract thought. Nin's sessions with Allendy, however, have led her to recognize that there is a positive side to the mental capacities commonly dismissed as feminine—that there is a special kind of feminine thinking men lack, the ability "to explain what I feel" (152). Nin gradually expands the gender-based distinction between intellectuality and feeling into an artistic credo. Her world of experience, she grasps, does not hinge on "vast deserts, universes, cosmologies" but on the "human" and "personal." She exclaims, "I do not want to enter impersonal, non-human worlds" (158). Not long before meeting Rank, she declares, "I am a woman first of all. . . . I am personal. I am essentially human, not intellectual. I do not understand abstract art. Only art born of love, passion, pain" (223).

Nin connects a distinctive feminine art with the distinctive feminine mentality. During Miller's and Nin's preoccupation with June, they both attempt to write about her. Nin reads Miller's account and, conscious of how much of June's character and behavior he has rendered, muses, "What was left for me to do? To go where Henry cannot go, into the Myth, into June's dreams, fantasies, into the poetry of June. To write as a woman, and as a woman only" (128). (It was this effort that resulted in *The House of Incest*.) Rank puts in perspective and authenticates Nin's discoveries about her nature as a woman and about the relationship between her womanhood and her strengths as an artist. Women, Rank explains, are closer in their thought and behavior to the emotional basis of life that men often deny. Their feelings and intuitions tap many of the underlying truths of experience: "They remained in touch with that mysterious region which we [analysts] are now opening up." And because this region is "mysterious" and is inexpressible in literally descriptive discourse, women express their understanding "in terms of symbols, through dreams and myths" (276). With the backing of Rank's explanation and validation of her felt knowledge, Nin moves from the semiapologetic tone of her earlier accounts of herself as woman and artist to a rhetoric of certainty and advocacy. "*It is the woman who has to speak*" (289; Nin's italics). Aware of the general disinclination of either men or women to accept the distinctive voice of the woman artist, she adds, "And it is not only the woman Anaïs who has to speak, but I who have to speak for many women" (289). Bolstered by Rank, Nin is now sure that the capacity of women to feel intuitively is not a weakness, as a male-dominated outlook supposes, but a source of strength, and that it is her calling not only to apply this insight in her own fiction of myth, symbol, and dream but to promote it as available to others.

Although Nin maintains a relationship with Miller during the period of her greatest involvement with Rank, it is clear that Rank has supplanted Miller within the courtship-marriage trope that charts Nin's journey in self-identification. Miller, early in the journey, has played the necessary roles of guide and leader, but his range of exploration has been limited—in Nin's more mature view—by his excessive physicality and his lack of responsiveness to the "mysteries" of the feminine nature. But in Rank she can find a "wise and courageous guide" and true "power and mastery" (284). Nin's relationship with Miller—in yet another familial trope—no longer positions him as a knowing and strong parent, with her as an inquiring child, but reduces him to someone in need of her strength and guidance. With Rank, on the other hand, she has recovered the satisfaction of possessing both a "lover" and a "father."

The *Diary* could end with an adequate effect of closure at this point, given Nin's twofold triumph in confirming herself as woman and artist and in establishing a deeply satisfying relationship with Rank. But Nin elects to include in the final portion of the *Diary* a full account of the stillbirth of her child in August, 1934, which in its pain, anguish, and sense of failure seems to run against the grain of the theme of a journey successfully accomplished.[16]

Nin's depiction of the stillbirth is horrific in its graphic detail and its exhibition of Nin's sense of guilt and failure. But there is more to the account than that. Nin has employed birth and motherhood as symbols of authorship at numerous earlier points in the *Diary*. For example, while working on *The Winter of Artifice* in early 1934—when she was about to become pregnant—she comments, "Writing now shows the pains of childbearing. No joy. Just pain, sweat, exhaustion. . . . I yearn to be delivered of this book. It is devouring me" (315). Rank has earlier discussed with Nin her desire to play roles pleasing to men and has sought to deflect her above all from her inclination to play the role of mother—"to protect, serve, mother, care for" (290). Given these opposing images of the woman artist as mother—that the woman can as artist experience the richness of giving birth, that the artist can as woman have her self-expression impeded by her motherly tendencies—the stillbirth of Nin's child takes on, paradoxically, an upward rather than downward direction. She has failed in her mother-

---

16. The father is not named in the *Diary*, but he is revealed to be Miller in Nin's *Incest* (San Diego, 1992), 329. Her decision not to name the father in the *Diary* no doubt springs from the same concern for protecting Miller's privacy that led her not to disclose their sexual relationship. But it is also possible to relate her omission of the identification to her earlier portrayal of the two prostitutes in the whorehouse in the rue Blondel. The fact of a father was less important for Nin than the fact of her childbearing, and the omission of a specific father dramatized this distinction.

hood, she feels initially, "or at least the embodiment of it," but there is left to her Lawrence' compelling "symbolic motherhood," that is, the artist's capacity to bring "hope into the world" (346). And as though to dramatize and confirm the powerful elegiac theme of a physical loss compensated for by a spiritual gain, there follows a striking mystical moment as Nin recovers in the hospital. As she lies in bed on a clear, sunny day, she feels a momentous sense of union with the physical universe and thus with God. "The light and the sky in the body. God in the body, and I melting into God. . . . I felt space, gold, purity, ecstasy, immensity, a profound ineluctable communion" (348).

On leaving the hospital, Nin is swept in a new direction. She has earlier, at the height of her enthusiasm for Rank and for the benefits of a humane and artist-centered form of analysis, decided to become a practitioner herself, and has studied for a time with Rank, at the University of Paris. Now Rank has decided to move to New York and seeks to persuade Nin to follow him there as his assistant. By this time, however, in the familiar pattern of the *Diary*, Nin has begun to with-draw from her "marriage" with Rank. She has recognized his human limitations—his want of humor and his overabstract frame of mind—and she has also, in her studies at the university, felt the sterility of the academic pursuit of analysis. What is more, Rank, like Miller and Allendy before him, has gone from being an instructor to being a supplicant for Nin's own strength and attention. Nin instinctively senses the transposing of roles as potentially imprisoning. Nevertheless, she decides that she will help Rank for a brief period, and with considerable excitement she is preparing for her move to New York as the *Diary* ends, in November, 1934, almost exactly three years after her initial entry.

Nin's account of these three years of growth within the Paris moment concludes with a climactic image that sums up the paradox at the heart of her development. She writes in the spring of 1934, as her relationship with Rank is losing its intensity,

> In the very center of the Carnival, I began to think of a Cathedral. An immense Cathedral loomed in the heart of my light joys, the opposite of flow. I used to build cathedrals, cathedrals of sentiment, for love, for love of men, for love as prayer, love as communion, with a great sense of continuity and detail and enduringness. Built against the flux and mobility of life, in defiance of it. Then with Henry, with June, with analysis, with Rank, I began to flow, not to build. Yesterday, flow seemed

so easy. Pure flow and enjoyment of life leave me thirsty. I began to think of Cathedrals. Why? I had the medieval faith needed for great constructions, the fervor and exaltation. I build up human relationships with divine care. With sacrifices, lies, deceptions, I build up continuity, permanence. (327)

Human relationships to Nin are cathedrals not only in their seeming permanence and solidity but also in their expression of the sacrament of love. Each of Nin's "marriages" is indeed a cathedral in its embodiment of the human need for grandeur and permanence and the expression of the deepest human feelings. Someone loves and therefore wishes and expects love to last for ever. But a corollary demand in life is for flow, for change, for journeys into fresh ranges of experiences through new personal relationships. So in the great paradox at the center of the themes and form of the *Diary*, the very edifice that at first appears to be a cathedral—with Miller or with June or with Rank—is dissolved within the flow that exists in dialectic tension with the desire for permanence. The final entry of the *Diary*, when Nin is preparing to join Rank in New York, therefore also expresses her need to push on past her relationship with him. "I cannot install myself anywhere yet," Nin concludes. "I must climb dizzier heights" (360).

Nin's *Diary* is a special case of the modernist "drama of consciousness."[17] That the consciousness here is Nin's own rather than that of a fictional character does not negate that Nin seeks to render the interior life. As in a late novel by Henry James, exterior events matter less than responses to events, and plot comes less from the interaction between character and event than from a consciousness' gradual accretion of understanding about the meaning of an event and about the nature of its own response to what has happened. Little of importance occurs externally in Nin's relationship to June and Allendy, for example, but she undergoes transformations of attitude toward the two figures, and it is variations of that kind which constitute the plot of the *Diary*.

This is not to say that the *Diary* is only interior analysis. Nin shrewdly varies her narrative style to achieve diversity of form and to profit from the special capabilities of particular styles. For example, Nin often introduces a highly charged event at a key moment of transition in her awareness or understanding, as James did in the famous scene in *The*

---

17. The phrase is from the preface Henry James wrote for the New York Edition of *Roderick Hudson* (New York, 1907), xvii.

Ambassadors of Strether encountering Chad and Madame de Vionnet on a country excursion. Among these are the whorehouse incident, the moment of Nin's showing her breasts to Allendy, the occasion when Henry and June are drunk and sick at Clichy, and the stillbirth of her child. The narrative frequently becomes documentary, as well, with letters from Miller or Artaud or Joaquin Nin, and occasionally it takes a dramatic tack, as when Nin casts her analytic sessions with Allendy in dialogue form. The *Diary* even contains a number of well-told inset tales—stories about figures in Nin's life which seem to be extraneous to her state of mind but which in fact often shed an oblique light on it. Thus Nin recollects finding a cache of pornographic books on first arriving in Paris, she tells about her Spanish dance instructor, and she goes into the details of Rank's early life.

Each chronologically designated section of the *Diary* not only encloses a body of material bearing on a major development in Nin's life during this period but also is shaped into the expressive vehicle best suited to her subject matter. Often the introduction to the section recounts a brief incident illustrating the relationship that is its theme: June's dramatic entrance at Louveciennes is an obvious example. The section is then divided into entries the topics and length of which are imitative of the relationships themselves. During the period Nin is deeply involved with Allendy, she also spends much time at the Clichy apartment of Henry Miller and Fred Perlès. The entries in this section alternate, often precisely, between Allendy's consulting room and the apartment as a representation of the two differing yet complementary ways in which Nin is undertaking her journey to freedom. When Nin is later seeing both Artaud and her father and realizes that both relationships amount to a kind of madness, the entries about them not only alternate but signify by their brevity a hectic impatience and a soon-to-be-achieved break with the figures. We have already seen that Nin's complete absorption in Rank is reflected in the length of the section devoted entirely to his ideas and her relationship with him.

Nin's ability to shape the *Diary* into a form of fiction is clear as well in her manipulation of the *Diary* itself as a character in her thoughts and development. Most obviously, the diary is Nin's secret self. It is, metaphorically, written in the dark and thus cannot serve as a mirror of the roles expected of her daytime persona. The Nin here portrayed, we are encouraged to believe, is the "true" Nin. And the authentic Nin is a woman of feeling, generosity of spirit, depth, and insight. She has weaknesses and foibles, but she is essentially a heroic adventurer in quest of the grail of selfhood, and the *Diary* as secret self holds the record of her effort. Collaterally, the *Diary* is therefore also a "travel sketchbook" (158) and "itinerary" (189) of a soul in transit. But it is, as well, a refuge from the difficulties and hardships of the passage and is therefore both a solace and a potential narcotic addiction (333).

It is as addictive escape that Nin's diary is something all her marriage partners, including the most understanding, Miller and Rank, try to persuade her to give up. Ostensibly they wish her to devote herself to her fiction, but all are also instinctively jealous of the diary as Nin's most "steadfast friend" (224)—as, in short, a rival lover. "All of them would slay the journal if they could," Nin ruefully notes (215). The *Diary* as secret and permanent friend thus adds another dimension to Nin's evocative dialectic about cathedrals and flux. She has established a permanent edifice expressive of her deepest self after all, but it exists not in an external relationship but in the *Diary* itself as a record of such relationships—in a word, in her art. Like the other expatriate writers, Nin has translated her pursuit of freedom within the Paris moment into a personal aesthetic. Freedom and creativity are at once the goals of Nin's life and the means by which she remakes her life into art. The *Diary* not only is a testament to a journey undertaken and achieved but also articulates that testament fully and movingly through the innovative art of the adventurer.

THE MOMENT IMAGINED AND
REMEMBERED: FICTION

Ernest Hemingway
The Sun Also Rises

I have thus far confined the discussion to autobiographies and journals. In that kind of writing, the obstetrical function of Paris is portrayed in a positive light. The birth is successfully concluded; indeed, the principal intent of each work is to depict the emergence and triumph of the creative imagination within a Paris context. But it should be clear as well that many of the major Paris scenes that I have discussed contain a darker side: the frustration in the "good café" of a girl longed for but not possessed, the complex emotions locked up within the walls of the unmentioned bedroom of the rue de Fleurus, the degradation of the spirit embodied by the prostitutes of the rue Blondel. It is in the fiction of the American expatriate writers of the period that the tragic potential in the effort to achieve a richness and intensity of creative expression within a Paris setting is fully explored and dramatized. In such scenes as the impotent Jake Barnes at the *bal musette,* or Richard Savage desperately seeking to escape the problem of Daughter's pregnancy, or Dick Diver caught in a Paris hotel between the competing claims of Nicole and Rosemary—in these scenes and situations the sexuality of the Paris moment is the symbolic analogue not of creative strength and freedom but of a bitterly ironic failure to achieve what is so urgently desired. The artist-manqué figures of Jake, Savage, and Dick, like Hemingway, Stein, and Nin in their self-portraits, seek a vital expression of selfhood, but now the sexuality of their worlds mocks rather than aids in the desired fulfillment.

Despite this difference between autobiography and fiction in the dramatization of the Paris moment, the close similarity between the expatriate experiences of Jake, Savage, and Dick, on the one hand, and those of Hemingway, Dos Passos, and Fitzgerald, on the other, reveals the powerful autobiographical foundation of almost all expatriate writing set abroad. All the novels I will examine rely heavily on their authors' lives in Europe for specifics of plot and characterization. *Tropic of Cancer* (if it is considered a novel) and *The Sun Also Rises* are explicitly autobiographical in dramatis personae and action. A minor scholarly industry exists in the roman à clef character of *The Sun Also Rises,* and *Tropic of Cancer* is baldly dependent on Miller's life, friends, and experience. *Tender Is the Night* and *Nineteen-Nineteen* are also deeply autobiographical but in a somewhat different way from *The Sun Also Rises* and *Tropic of Cancer,* in that their protagonists derive from the personal experiences of other expatriate figures as well as of their authors.

Of course, fiction often has autobiographical roots, and during the 1920s and 1930s the theme of the alienated self—as in the work of Thomas Wolfe—encouraged a fiction of self-dramatization. But expatriate fiction constitutes a special kind of autobiographical fiction in both the intensity and the fullness of its reliance on the author's personal experience—characteristics that suggest the overwhelming primacy of expatriation in the lives and thoughts of its authors. A writer may or may not turn to his recent move from Chicago to New York or from the city to the suburbs for the subject matter of his next novel, but few authors could escape the impact of expatriation on their attention. So deeply felt was the act of self-exile that it seemed to demand translation into meaning and form.

Two interrelated questions arise out of the relationship between the autobiographically based expatriate novel in which a potentially creative self is frustrated and defeated and the memoir in which there is a rich flowering of the artist on foreign soil. Why does the expatriate experience lend itself to this thematic dichotomy, and why does the dichotomy find an outlet in these two distinctive forms? Writers such as Hemingway, Fitzgerald, Dos Passos, and Miller saw all around them in the cafés and streets of Paris countless examples among their compatriots of inadequacy and weakness, ranging from bohemian dilettantism to a perversion of the opportunity for freedom into self-destruction and the destruction of others. They, however—Hemingway with his superb sense of personal worth and destiny, Miller with his exuberant base of romantic ego and role, and Fitzgerald and Dos Passos with major and successful work already accomplished—viewed themselves as apart, as different, as capable, in short, of drawing upon the creative potency of the Paris moment rather than succumbing to its faculty for corrupting further an already vitiated or flawed spirit and will.

The memoir and the novel are forms aptly positioned to render the distinction between self-vision and the observation of others within a body of shared experience. The memoir, for the writer, is principally a vehicle for expressing his conception of how he grew into creative identity and competence. Fiction, because of the immediate and inherent distance between author and subject—whatever the autobiographical origins of the subject—can be a vehicle for exhibiting the tragic failure of others to achieve similar growth. And in both literary forms the same Paris matrix of scene and event can yield the symbolic analogue of what a writer or a fictional protagonist is or is not becoming. Put somewhat differently, the memoir permits the artist to trace the birth and triumph of a vocation; the novel permits him to dramatize, and thus possibly to exorcise, his worst fears about himself as an artist through the depiction of figures resembling himself yet essentially different as well. Hemingway is not impotent and Dos Passos is not a moral coward, despite the fact that Jake Barnes and Richard Savage reprise much in their authors' expatriate experience. And Fitzgerald, despite resembling Dick Diver in many ways, did not retreat defeated into a living death but rather sought to return to creative well-being through the depiction of his own collapse.

The expatriate novels under consideration rely on their authors' Paris moment to express a tragic rather than a triumphant vision of experience. In fiction as in autobiography Paris is indeed only an obstetrical instrument. Protagonists bring to the city their origins—their flaws and limitations of character—which then flourish in the city's climate of freedom. The American abroad is thus often portrayed satirically, because of his gauche falsification of the ideals of freedom and creativity (as by Hemingway in Robert Cohn and by Miller in Van Norden), or with tragic pathos, because of his inability to free himself from a particular incubus of selfhood despite the deeply appealing possibility of doing so within the expatriate experience (as in Jake Barnes and Dick Diver).

Another striking difference between expatriate fiction and autobiography lies in the extent to which Paris serves as the setting in each form. Aside from Stein's depiction of her wartime experiences and summer excursions and Nin's few ventures outside her Paris locale, the three memoirs I have dealt with are confined to Paris and accordingly focus the reader's attention on the significance of Parisian life in the blossoming of the author. The novels I will examine, however, though set in Europe either entirely (*The Sun Also Rises* and *Tender Is the Night*) or largely (*Nineteen-Nineteen*), take place only partly in Paris, ranging from the relatively brief portion of *Tender Is the Night*—about a fifth of the work—to approximately half of *Nineteen-Nineteen*. (*Tropic of Cancer,* however, aside from the brief sections placed in Le Havre and Dijon, is entirely set in Paris.) The major portions of each novel occurring outside Paris of course require non-Parisian settings for specific purposes: the Burguete and Pamplona sections of *The Sun Also Rises,* for example, the Riviera chapters of *Tender Is the Night,* and the American portions of *Nineteen-Nineteen*. But I will argue that the Paris moment plays an especially important part in each novel as a whole by exploiting the resonance of the mythic Paris of creative fecundity to crystallize characterization and theme. My greatest attention will therefore be on the Paris scenes: on Jake Barnes in Paris before the Pamplona trip; on Dick Savage, Eveline, and Daughter thrown together in Paris during and after the war; on the Divers and Rosemary coming up to Paris from Antibes. The Paris scenes in these novels pointedly sum up the major themes of the works, I shall argue, as well as express the principal conventions in the fictional characterization of the Paris moment.

The Sun Also Rises is one of the most examined novels in American literary history, with a recent bibliography listing over 150 essays on the work between 1974 and 1989.[1] A number of approaches to the novel— its sources in the events of the summer of 1925, its relationship to T. S. Eliot's symbols and themes of sterility, its dramatization of a Hemingway-code hero, and its symbolic form—have been touched upon so many times from so many angles that they have the familiarity of folk wisdom. Recently, as a result of the publication of Hemingway's *The Garden of Eden* in 1986, biographical critics have been mining the novel seeking to identify Hemingway's personal gender politics in Brett Ashley and Jake Barnes.[2] My own approach will be to concentrate on the Paris portion of the novel as a paradigm or microcosm of the novel

1. Kelli A. Larson, *Ernest Hemingway: A Reference Guide, 1974–1989* (Boston, 1991).

2. See especially Kenneth S. Lynn, *Hemingway* (New York, 1987); Mark Spilka, *Hemingway's Quarrel with Androgyny* (Lincoln, Nebr., 1990); and James R. Mellow, *Hemingway: A Life Without Consequences* (Boston, 1992).

as a whole—a method that will, I hope, cast some new light both on those scenes and on the entire work.[3]

Because the Paris scenes of *The Sun Also Rises* seem to flow one into the other, forming a seamless whole, it is not often realized that this part of the novel has a distinctive internal structure, describable as a prologue followed by three acts. The prologue consists of Chapter I and part of Chapter II, where we meet Robert Cohn through Jake's recounting of their friendship. That is followed (act one, beginning in Chapter II) by the narration of an afternoon and evening during which Jake works, picks up a prostitute, has dinner with her, attends a *bal musette* and encounters Brett near the place de la Contrescarpe, visits a Montparnasse café with Brett, and goes home alone—though Brett also joins him briefly before he goes to sleep. The next day (act two, the opening of Chapter V), Jake has lunch with Cohn but spends most of the day working. In the evening, after being stood up by Brett at the Hôtel Crillon, he goes to Montparnasse and finds himself enmeshed in Cohn's difficulties with his mistress, Frances Clyne. He escapes to his apartment, where Brett again comes to see him, this time bringing with her Count Mippipopulous, who accompanied her the evening before but did not come upstairs. The three go out to dinner and to a Montmartre nightclub, and then Jake again returns home alone. The end of the second day closes Chapter VII and Book I. Chapter VIII and Book II open a week or so later (act three) with a brief recapitulation of Jake's activities during the interval but then shift into a narration of yet another Paris day. Jake's friend Bill Gorton arrives in Paris. They accidentally meet Brett on their way to dinner on the Ile Saint-Louis but dine alone and then walk from the Seine to Montparnasse, where they once more encounter Brett, accompanied by her fiancé, Mike Campbell. The chapter and evening close with Jake and Bill attending a prizefight together. Chapter IX begins with the brief scene of Jake, Brett, and Mike at a Montparnasse bar but then quickly shifts to Jake and Bill leaving for Pamplona a few days later.

The Paris scenes of *The Sun Also Rises* are carefully orchestrated to

3. Much commentary on *The Sun Also Rises* touches upon the Paris setting of the novel. Studies that have proved useful for my purposes include Jean Méral's *Paris in American Literature* (Chapel Hill, N.C., 1989); George Morgan's "An American in Paris: Strategies of Otherness in *The Sun Also Rises*," *CYCNOS*, II (1985–86), 27–39; Michael S. Reynolds' *Hemingway: The Paris Years* (Oxford, 1989) and *The Sun Also Rises: A Novel of the Twenties* (Boston, 1988); Frederic J. Svoboda's *Hemingway and "The Sun Also Rises": The Crafting of a Style* (Lawrence, Kans., 1983); and Arnold E. Davidson and Cathy N. Davidson's "Decoding the Hemingway Hero in *The Sun Also Rises*," in *New Essays on "The Sun Also Rises,"* ed. Linda Wagner-Martin (New York, 1987).

highlight specific qualities of the Paris moment. Jake and Cohn make their appearance as figures embodying contrasting expatriate value systems, both of which, however, are flawed. The qualities associated with each figure are then extended into the Paris cityscape, characters, and events over a repetitive yet progressive three-day cycle. Each of the days is structured around a journey during which Jake moves between such resonant Paris sites as the Pantheon district, Montparnasse cafés and bars, and the Ile Saint-Louis and the Seine. As Jake goes from distinctive place to distinctive place, the three days form themselves into a rich image of the expatriate experience—its emptiness and futility and yet its potential to refresh and renew.

Jake and Robert Cohn have become friends in a way typical of expatriates, inasmuch as they are drawn together more by being Americans abroad than by any similarity of temperament and values. They play tennis and bridge together, share meals, plan trips, and discuss the general situation of Americans in Europe. Aside from such superficial ties, the two are vastly different. Jake is a working newspaperman who is earning his way in Europe. He speaks the language, knows the people, and avoids bohemian hangouts. Jake has been injured in the war—a genital wound that has left him incapable of sexual intercourse. He likes his life abroad—Paris is a "good town" and he is enthusiastic about the bullfights and fishing in Spain—but he has no illusions that his expatriation will recreate him, will make him whole again physically, emotionally, and spiritually after the personal devastation that the war has wreaked upon him.[4] As he assures Cohn, "Going to another country doesn't make any difference. I've tried all that. You can't get away from yourself by moving from one place to another. There's nothing to that" (11).

Cohn, by contrast, retains a romantic faith in the power of transplantation, even though it has not worked for him in France. He has come to Paris, though he does not know the language and is not interested in the people, because it is the place for a young writer to be. Once there, he frequents the cafés of Montparnasse, acquires a mistress, and works sporadically on his novel while drawing a generous allowance from home. This mimicking of the life of the bohemian expatriate he performs with a hollow anxiety about getting it right—he senses that he is not—which leads him to think about other locations for romantic self-fulfillment. We find him in the opening chapter trying to persuade Jake to take a prolonged trip to South America with him.

---

4. *The Sun Also Rises* (1926; rpr. New York, 1957), 11. Further citations of this edition will appear in the text.

Jake and Cohn are thus from the start polar opposites within the expatriate experience. The worker who has paid and is still paying for what he is capable of enjoying in Europe is juxtaposed to the Montparnasse dilettante who seeks to ape the superficial trappings of the expatriate artist. (This distinction, of course, resurfaces as a controlling ethic in *A Moveable Feast*.) Yet the two figures are in one respect fundamentally similar, as is implied by Jake's fondness for Cohn and Cohn's pursuit of Jake's friendship, in that both have a limited capacity to fulfill the expatriate myth of creative renewal within the fecund freedom of the Paris moment. The various threads of the expatriate experience that come together in Jake and Cohn are overtly expressed in a conversation between Jake and Bill Gorton at Burguete, when Bill facetiously identifies Jake with Cohn's bohemian form of expatriation:

"You're an expatriate. You've lost touch with the soil. You get precious. Fake European standards have ruined you. You drink yourself to death. You become obsessed by sex. You spend all your time talking, not working. You are an expatriate, see? You hang around cafés."

"It sounds like a swell life," I said. "When do I work?"

"You don't work. One group claims women support you. Another group claims you're impotent."

"No," I said. "I just had an accident." (115)

Bill's comic placing of Jake within the popular stereotype of the expatriate of course pertains more to Cohn than to Jake and thus serves to distinguish Jake from the phoniness and role playing of the stereotype. Jake has not lost touch with the soil—he fishes and swims and enjoys bullfights—and he works hard. But he often does drink a great deal, and he is obsessed with sex in his anguish over his sexual incapacity. What is at issue here, however, is less the bohemian superstructure of the expatriate myth than Hemingway's belief, here expressed in its negative symbolic form, in the capacity of the Paris of food and drink to fuel the surrogate sexuality of creative expression and thus assure a measure of spiritual well-being. In Jake's case this circuit of productivity is broken not by the superficiality of Paris life but by his wound in all its symbolic force. He is not like Cohn, but he shares with Cohn a fundamental incapacity, in that both are unable to fulfill the potential of the Paris moment. Jake, as we find him at the opening of the novel, lacks a base of values or faith on which to structure a re-creation of himself into spiritual potency. He is thus limited to a dry and self-tormenting nibbling at the edge of the Paris moment that had nourished

Stein and Nin and Hemingway himself in *A Moveable Feast*—of drinking that produces only hangovers and of sexual longings that cannot be
satisfied.

Jake's first journey through a Paris day and cityscape—the first act
in the Paris three-act structure I mentioned earlier—renders Paris as a
spiritual wasteland. Jake, alone in a café on the Right Bank, invites a
prostitute, Georgette, to have a drink with him and then amuses himself
by taking her to a restaurant for dinner. When she seeks to engage him
sexually in a horse cab, he puts her off, admitting that he is "sick." Her
reply is, "Everybody's sick. I'm sick, too" (16). At the restaurant they
encounter a group including Cohn and his mistress and the novelist
Braddocks and his wife, who invite Jake to a private dance at a *bal
musette* on the rue Montagne Sainte-Geneviève, not far from the place
de la Contrescarpe.

As Georgette says, "Everybody's sick," and nowhere more so than at
the thickly textured scene of the *bal musette,* in which every overt and
implicit sexual strand contributes to a theme of spiritual frustration and
failure. Georgette and Jake illustrate not only the obvious association of
male impotence and female prostitution with sexual inadequacy but also
Hemingway's belief that homosexuality is a brand of sexual failure. Jake
facetiously introduces Georgette to Mrs. Braddocks as Georgette Le-
blanc, a well-known lesbian singer, and Jake's name conjoins playfully
the names of Natalie Barney and Djuna Barnes, two expatriate American lesbians, with the street on which was located Barney's lesbian
salon, the rue Jacob.[5] The whole scale of sexual taint, as Hemingway
conceives it, is thus touched upon by the two figures: venereal disease
("Im sick, too," Georgette has reported), prostitution, impotence, and
homosexuality.

The *bal musette,* once all its participants are present—Brett arrives
unexpectedly, accompanied by a group of homosexuals—is a parody
of the Capulet ball in *Romeo and Juliet.* In both, two lovers meet
accidentally at a dance. But in *The Sun Also Rises,* instead of the mix
of youthful sexual innocence and eagerness that pervades the moment
in Shakespeare, all is sexual falseness and incompleteness as the sexual
roles displayed approach the range of depiction in a Hogarth caricature.
There is impotence (Jake), male homosexuality (the novelist Prentiss
and the young men with Brett), a nymphomaniac availability with a
touch of lesbianism (Brett, who "like[d] to add them up" and whose
hair is "brushed back like a boy's"; 23, 22), prostitution (Georgette),

5. Lynn, *Hemingway,* 323.

and simple lust (Cohn, once Brett arrives). Hemingway has saturated the scene with sexual behavior and attitudes that to his mind lack honesty and completeness. There will never be either triumphant fulfillment or tragic grandeur in these lives, he implies, only the pathos of a vast impotence of the spirit.

Jake and Brett appear to possess some means of escape from the implications of the *bal musette,* since they are in love. So they shed their "false" companions—Georgette and the homosexuals who arrived with Brett—and leave together in a taxi. But there all the frustrations of their longing for each other come to the surface—"Oh, darling, I've been so miserable," Brett says (24)—and their movement through Paris in the taxi provides no true mobility or change. There is no place for an act of fulfillment of self for them—no "good café," no salon of like-minded creative spirits, no train ride to Clichy to join a loved one— only a long and desultory taxi ride to the Sélect in Montparnasse, a major symbol in Hemingway's reservoir of Parisian images of bohemian emptiness. There, hammering home the theme of desire without fruition and movement without mobility, they find the very crowd from the *bal musette.* Jake soon leaves and walks back to his apartment near the Luxembourg Gardens. He too is miserable, and in the privacy of his bedroom and the dark begins to cry. Brett appears, drunk, and attempts to persuade him to join her and a Greek-American "count" she has just met. Jake declines, and feeling "like hell again" (34), tries to sleep.

The second act—the next day—begins like the first, with Jake at work, to be joined by Cohn, who now reveals his infatuation with Brett—not Brett as she is but rather the well-bred British member of the nobility of his romantic imagination. After finishing work, Jake is stood up by Brett at the Crillon, on the Right Bank, and makes his way to the Sélect, expecting to find her there. Instead, he is trapped into listening as Frances Clyne relentlessly attacks Cohn. The long passage concerning Frances' harangue—more than half of Chapter VI—is the symbolic equivalent of the *bal musette* scene of the previous act. There the emphasis had been on the segment of the expatriate experience represented by Jake and Brett—of those who paid their dues and are seeking a desperate gaiety in compensation. The scene with Cohn and Frances at the Dôme—they have crossed the boulevard from the Sélect—captures a different but analogous emptiness of spirit. Cohn is in a relationship with Frances not because he was deeply drawn to her but because he knows that an expatriate writer is supposed to have a mistress. But now a more compelling possibility of playing to

The Café Dôme in the twenties

type appears to have arisen—the possibility of an affair with a British noblewoman—and he is ready to disencumber himself of Frances even if it means paying her off. Frances, for her part, is bitter and angry and lights into Cohn without mercy. Cohn, she asserts, is searching for romance in his life in order to have material for his fiction. "So now he's going out and get some new material" (50) because "if he marries me, like he's always promised he would, that would be the end of all the romance" (51).

Jake is embarrassed and appalled by Frances' diatribe, as he was by Brett's arrival at the *bal musette* accompanied by homosexuals, and again he seeks to escape. Again he goes home, and again Brett arrives with the count in tow. This time, though, she and the count remain for some time. In the final important scene of the second act, a new note is struck, one that will be even more fully sounded during the third and last day that we follow Jake through Paris.

The count, an older man, has great wealth, which he displays ostentatiously and which is of dubious origin. (A parallel with Fitzgerald's Gatsby is apparent.) But there is more to the count than the conventionally comic figure of an overage roué who has offered Brett a large sum to join him in Biarritz. The count's philosophy of life, which he explains to Jake and Brett, makes explicit the theme of paying implicit in the depiction of their own lives. His beliefs begin to emerge in his comments on the "amazing" champagne he has brought with him. Brett offers a toast, and he replies, "This wine is too good for toast-drinking, my dear. You don't want to mix emotions up with a wine like that. You lose the taste." All he wants of wines, he concludes, "is to enjoy them" (59). Later, in a mock contest with Jake over who has been "around" the most, he declares that he has been in seven wars and three revolutions, including a conflict in Abyssinia in which he received arrow wounds. He displays the wounds, and Brett observes to Jake, "I told you he was one of us" (60).

The count, unlike Cohn but like Jake and Brett—who has lost her first husband in the war and who earlier remarks to Jake, "Don't we pay for all the things we do" (26)—has had a difficult life and suffered real wounds. But unlike Jake and Brett, he has found a way to engage life pleasurably despite his wounds—despite his physical scars and the psychological and emotional injuries they also stand for—by discounting them in the present, by not mixing up emotion in the concrete satisfying abundance of the moment. "It is because I have lived very much that I can now enjoy everything so well" (60). Jake heartily agrees, but his concurrence is at this point only token. The champagne is excellent, the count is good company, and he is enjoying himself, but there is still the deep hurt of his wound as an underlying pain and frustration. The second day therefore ends much as the first. After dinner in the Bois, the three go to a nightclub in Montmartre. But Jake and Brett are again "miserable." He sees her home to her hotel and returns to his apartment alone. Still, the count has planted a seed—one that will be further cultivated during the third act of Jake's Paris moment and will come to fruition later in the novel. It is possible, perhaps not always and for all people but at any rate sometimes and for some people, to grasp and consume and profit from the spirit-fulfilling physical activities at the heart of life—in short, to "enjoy" them—so long as one has paid in advance to do so.

The third act of the Paris sections of *The Sun Also Rises* does not follow immediately upon the second. Cohn disappears, and Brett is in San Sebastian: they are together, of course, as Jake later learns. Jake remains in Paris to work. After a week or so of this interval, the act begins with the arrival of Bill Gorton in Paris. Gorton, a successful writer who relishes life fully, confirms the operative ethic of the count within the Paris scene. And since he occupies Jake's attention the entire third day, and does so, in his enthusiasm for Paris and his anticipation of the fishing and bullfighting that are to come, in ways closely related to Jake's own distinctive capacity to enjoy, his presence and his camaraderie with Jake introduce firmly into the Paris moment the dual theme of the work as a whole: that Jake's generation is deeply flawed but that life continues to offer, even for it, sustaining riches.

On the third day (which occupies the first chapter of Book II), we are, as on the first and second days, taken on a journey through Paris. This time, however, the journey does not lead through the moral chaos of the crowd at the *bal musette* or through Frances' vicious berating of Cohn at the Dôme, but rather takes in a Paris of natural calm and beauty. Jake and Bill begin by walking from Jake's apartment to the river in order to dine on the Ile Saint-Louis. They have a good meal at a small restaurant and then walk along the Seine.

> The river was dark and a bateau mouche went by, all bright with lights, going fast and quiet up and out of sight under the bridge. Down the river was Notre Dame squatting against the night sky. We crossed to the left bank of the Seine by the wooden foot-bridge from the Quai de Berthune, and stopped on the bridge and looked down the river at Notre Dame. Standing on the bridge the island looked dark, the houses were high against the sky, and the trees were shadows.
> "It's pretty grand," Bill said. "God, I love to get back." (77)

The passage expresses a romantic paradox similar to that of Wordsworth's "Composed upon Westminster Bridge," where the "Ships, towers, domes, theatres, and temples" of London take on, in the early morning calm, the transcendent loveliness of a natural scene. "Earth has not anything to show more fair," Wordsworth begins his poem. And as though to ratify the healing property of the moment on the bridge and thus the regenerative capacity of all nature, as Bill and Jake are observing the river, "a man and girl passed us. They were walking with their arms around each other" (77)—an image of "natural" affection and love sharply at odds with the "unnatural" sexuality of the *bal musette* and the sexual warfare of the Dôme.

The scene thus enlarges on the ethic that the count introduced. There the stress was on payment—on earning through the pain and anguish of experience the right to enjoy what life can still provide. The pain was real, but the enjoyment—the "amazing" wine, the good dinner in the Bois, the congenial company of the count—were also real. Now, in the third act, attention turns to a special kind of reality for those who have paid and are seeking respite and possible renewal—

that of nature in its eternal beauty and flow. Even in the heart of Paris, one can encounter the wealth of this permanent aspect of experience and respond strongly to it.

The two complementary ethics Jake experiences during the three acts (or journeys) of the Paris moment of *The Sun Also Rises* powerfully inform the themes and structure of the remainder of the novel. During the "war" (146), "explosion" (152), and "nightmare" (222) of the Pamplona *feria*—metaphors linking it both to Jake's combat experience and to the sexual impotence and warfare of the *bal musette* and the Dôme—Jake again encounters the sharp cleavage between those who have paid (his own group, including Brett, Mike Campbell, and Bill) and those who have not (principally Cohn). Forced to seek answers by the combined and heightened ugliness and emptiness of both groups, Jake articulates fully and with an explicit moral conclusion the metaphor and ethic of payment he has absorbed from his Paris journeys:

> I thought I had paid for everything. . . . You paid some way for everything that was any good. I paid my way into enough things that I liked, so that I had a good time. . . . It seemed like a fine philosophy. In five years, I thought, it will seem just as silly as all the other fine philosophies I've had.
>
> Perhaps that wasn't true, though. Perhaps as you went along you did learn something. I did not care what it was all about. All I wanted to know was how to live in it. Maybe if you found out how to live in it you learned from that what it was all about.
>
> I wished Mike would not behave so terribly to Cohn, though. Mike was a bad drunk. . . . Mike was unpleasant after he passed a certain point. I liked to see him hurt Cohn. I wished he would not do it, though, because afterward it made me disgusted at myself. That was morality; things that made you disgusted afterward. No, that was immorality. (148–49)

This discourse, which begins with a summary of the "philosophy" of payment, of the earned capacity to enjoy, and closes with an extension of the philosophy into the question of what kinds of enjoyment are moral and immoral, receives its fullest dramatic illustration in the nature and actions of the young bullfighter Pedro Romero. For if Jake is the wounded and thus impotent artist of his time who is able to enjoy only as an act of relief, Romero is the complementary potent artist of the present and the future who evokes beauty out of his creative strength, who makes us see that aesthetic pleasure is possible in the act of paying.

Romero, as we learn from Jake, does not fake his close encounters with death while fighting but confronts them with grace and beauty. With many bullfighters, "afterward, all that was faked turned bad and gave an unpleasant feeling. Romero's bull-fighting gave real emotion" (168). Romero is the bold and honest spirit that each of the "lost" group might have been but for their horrible wounds. The sexual metaphors of physical, spiritual, and artistic potency join positively in Romero not only in the plotting of the conclusion of the *feria,* when he "defeats" Cohn and beds Brett, but also in his combat with his last bull. "The bull wanted it again. . . . Each time [Romero] let the bull pass so close that the man and the bull and the cape that filled and pivoted ahead of the bull were all one sharply etched mass. It was all so slow and so controlled" (217).

In addition, the shape of the remainder of the novel following the Paris scenes—the shift from the cleansing days at Burguete, when Jake and Bill recapitulate and extend the transcendent moment on the Seine, to the Montparnasse-like sexual emptiness and combat of Pamplona, and then to another cleansing, on the beach at San Sebastian—echoes the rhythmic pattern of the three acts in Paris, in which Jake moves continuously from the Paris of anger and frustration to that of enjoyment. Indeed, the patterns reach similar conclusions in both portions of the novel. In the closing passages of the third and last act in Paris, Jake and Bill leave the river and walk to Montparnasse and the Sélect. There they find Mike and Brett and so are back in the Paris of the walking wounded, just as at the close of the novel Jake will be called from his haven of San Sebastian to rejoin an anguished Brett in Madrid. The sun also rises, Hemingway makes clear, but for those with an incurable sickness of the spirit there are only momentary respites.

John Dos Passos
Nineteen-Nineteen

With Dos Passos' *Nineteen-Nineteen,* as with Nin's *Diary,* there are initial obstacles to considering the book an expatriate work. For one, the novel is linked in its larger themes to the first and last novels in the

U.S.A. trilogy, *The 42nd Parallel* and *The Big Money,* neither of which is set in Europe. For another, *Nineteen-Nineteen* itself contains major strands—the Joe Williams and Ben Compton narratives, for example, and several of the biographies—that have little to do with its Paris-based material. In addition, the modernist experimental form of the work—its four distinctive alternating modes, from fictional narratives and mock biographies to collections of newspaper fragments and autobiographical Camera Eye stream-of-consciousness passages, which shift radically in place and time from mode to mode—seems to preclude an emphasis on a specific setting. And finally, because the action of the novel occurs principally between 1917 and 1919, it seems to take place too early to bear significantly on the expatriate experience. For these reasons the work seldom appears in discussions of expatriate writing.

Nineteen-Nineteen is, however, a major work of expatriate expression within the broad conception of the form which I have adopted for this study. Most of the central portion of the work—once the early Joe Williams narratives decline in frequency and before there is a return to the American scene at the close of the novel—is set in Paris, not only in the narratives of Richard Ellsworth Savage, Eveline Hutchins, and Daughter but in the experience of the Camera Eye persona and in the lives and events depicted in the biographies and Newsreels. As Dos Passos was to recall, after the armistice of late 1918 and with the onset of the peace conference at Versailles in January, 1919, Paris, in the spring of 1919, became the "capital of the world."[1] Dos Passos signified this union of time, place, and importance by naming the novel *Nineteen-Nineteen* even though much of its action occurs during 1917 and 1918, and by his early pictorial working plan for it, the "Geography of *Nineteen Nineteen,*" which depicts Paris as the center of a hub, with spokes radiating out to New York, Alsace, Rome, and Constantinople.[2] It is one aspect of Dos Passos' translation of this conception into fictional terms that three of the five narrative figures of *Nineteen-Nineteen* (Savage, Eveline, and Daughter) and three of the narrative figures initially introduced in *The 42nd Parallel* (Janey Williams, J. Ward Moorehouse, and Eleanor Stoddard)—the six coming from widely different backgrounds

---

1. Dos Passos, *The Best Times: An Informal Memoir* (New York, 1966), 76.
2. The sketch is also reproduced in Donald Pizer's *Dos Passos' "U.S.A.": A Critical Study* (Charlottesville, Va., 1988) following p. 95. Dos Passos later dropped Alsace and Constantinople as settings.

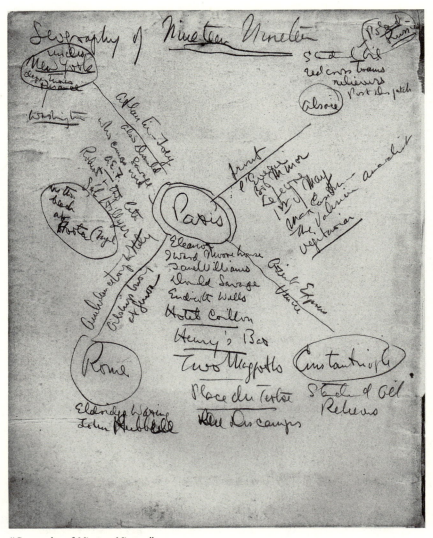

"Geography of *Nineteen-Nineteen*"
John Dos Passos Papers (# 5950-J), Special Collections Department, University of Virginia Library. Used by permission of Elizabeth Dos Passos.

and sections of the country—meet and intertwine their destinies in Paris during the spring of the city's ascendancy.

Dos Passos' designation of Paris as the capital of the world during the peace conference is in part sardonic, for he believed that the conference exemplified the duplicitous and narrow self-interest of postwar society in general. He conveyed this, however, not by depicting the conference itself—indeed, we never see it in session—but rather by portraying the personal lives of a group of Americans temporarily residing in Paris. Although this is a large group—far more than the six figures I have named—the most central and fully portrayed is Richard Savage, a young Harvard graduate and poet. Closely related to Savage in thematic significance is another young Harvard graduate and writer, the Camera Eye persona. By concentrating on the role of the Paris moment in crystallizing the essential natures of two American artists, Dos Passos has indeed entered the domain of expatriate fiction. Although he is more consciously and openly political and ideological than Hemingway and Fitzgerald, and although he is more fully responsive to cubist imperatives and thus arrives at a more discontinuous and fragmented rendering of the Paris scene than they, he is, like them, seeking to identify through the depiction of distinctive American sensibilities in Paris some of the major characteristics of the American experience of his time.

Dos Passos was graduated from Harvard in 1916 and arrived in Paris in late June, 1917, as a volunteer in the Norton-Harjes ambulance corps.[3] After a brief stay in the city and some training, he served at the front until his unit disbanded in early September. He left the city again in mid-November, going to Italy with an American Red Cross ambulance unit. After seven months in northern Italy, he was dismissed from the unit for his open antagonism toward the war. Back in America, he enlisted in the Army Medical Corps in October, 1918, and was on his way overseas when the war ended in November, 1918. In March, 1919, he was transferred to the Sorbonne Detachment, a group of American soldiers studying at the University of Paris. He was discharged from the army in July, 1919.

What is remarkable about Dos Passos' personal experiences between 1917 and 1919 is that they inform not only the consciously autobiographical figure of the Camera Eye but also—with the addition of borrowings from the background and peace-conference service of Dos Passos' Harvard classmate Robert Hillyer—the fictional figure of Richard Savage.[4] Both figures are Harvard graduates with literary aspirations

3. The major biographies of Dos Passos are Townsend Ludington's *John Dos Passos: A Twentieth-Century Odyssey* (New York, 1980) and Virginia Spencer Carr's *Dos Passos: A Life* (Garden City, N.Y., 1984).

4. Hillyer, a poet, was also a member of Dos Passos' ambulance unit and served with him at Verdun. There the two young men began a jointly written novel that attacked American middle-class failings and more specifically the war itself. Hillyer returned to America in the fall of 1917 and became an army officer. Stationed in Paris during the peace conference, he was a frequent army courier to other European cities. By the early 1930s—during Dos Passos' most radical years,

who join the ambulance corps, serve at Verdun and in Italy, and observe the peace conference while in the army. The similarity between the two is not the result of authorial laziness or of a failure of imagination but rather provides Dos Passos with the means to dramatize the twofold potential for the American artist in a time of national spiritual crisis. The artist can either rebel against the dominant and destructive ethos of his time and go down to seeming defeat (like the Camera Eye) or he can accommodate to the ethos and thus seemingly advance (like Savage).

Dos Passos had included in his early novel of army life, *Three Soldiers* (1921), a rough-hewn but powerful portrait of the part Paris could play in the life of an American artist seeking to escape the destructive lies of American life. John Andrews, a young Harvard-educated composer serving in France as an enlisted man, is crushed in spirit by the brutal regimentation of military life. Embittered as well by the deceptions and hypocrisy he finds in the pursuit of war aims, he comes to believe that "civilization [is] nothing but a vast edifice of sham, and the war, instead of its crumbling, was its fullest and most ultimate expression."[5] Seeking honesty, freedom, and creativity at all costs, he without permission leaves his unit for Paris. There, in Montmartre, he reflects, "What a wonderful life [it] would be to live up here in a small room that would overlook the great rosy grey expanse of the city . . . and to spend all your spare time working and going to concerts. . . . A quiet mellow existence . . . Think of my life beside it. Slaving in that iron, metallic, brazen New York . . . God! And this."[6]

Despite its overwrought and simplistic expression—*Three Soldiers* was written shortly after Dos Passos' discharge from the army—the depiction here of the American artist's relation to Paris anticipates its more successful representation in *Nineteen-Nineteen*. In both works, a world of deception, greed, and ruthless power, symbolized most immediately by the army and the war but characteristic also of American economic and social life in general, is juxtaposed against the world of freedom and creative fulfillment that Paris represents. The artist, both more responsive to and more in need of the richness of life, stands poised

---

when he was writing *Nineteen-Nineteen*—Hillyer had found what seemed to Dos Passos a safe berth within the establishment as a Harvard instructor and a conventional minor poet. Hillyer's early rebellion followed by an acceptance of conformity thus provided Dos Passos with a career pattern initially roughly parallel to that of the Camera Eye but eventually clearly divergent. See also Pizer, *Dos Passos' "U.S.A.,"* 143–44.

5. Dos Passos, *Three Soldiers* (1921; rpr. New York, 1962), 210.

6. *Ibid.,* 236.

between accepting imprisonment of the spirit within the system—the army in wartime, New York afterward—for the rewards the system provides, or rebelling against the system and thus going down to eventual defeat.

Nineteen-Nineteen is more compelling and evocative in rendering this theme, partly because of the devices Dos Passos employs to prevent an overidentification of himself with his characters. The want of distance between Dos Passos and John Andrews had produced much of the obviousness and stridency of *Three Soldiers*. The Camera Eye is openly autobiographical, but emotionalism is kept in check both by Dos Passos' ironic stance toward the figure and by his stream-of-consciousness symbolism. And his strategy of depicting the American presence in Paris by means of the modernist technique of multiplicity, in which various strands of narrative, biography, Newsreel, and Camera Eye touch upon different aspects of the Paris moment, helps create a rich tapestry of expatriate themes rather than a single-dimensional stress on the artist as a sensitive young man, as in the Andrews portion of *Three Soldiers*.[7] Richard Savage and the Camera Eye appear in a full context of other figures and events within the Paris scene, almost all of which also have relevance to their own character and experience. Juxtapositional implication—the consequence of seeing Savage and the Camera Eye in their relationship not only to each other but to the other Paris-centered narrative figures and to the careers and events depicted in the biographies and Newsreels—deepens and strengthens the portrayal of the Paris moment. Moreover, the experimental modal richness of *Nineteen-Nineteen*—as will be true as well of *Tropic of Cancer*—permits the work to bridge autobiography and fiction. As in an expatriate autobiography, *Nineteen-Nineteen* depicts in the Camera Eye the growth of a sensibility within the Paris scene, and as in an expatriate novel, it exhibits, in Richard Savage, a self-destructive failure to achieve that growth.

Nineteen-Nineteen opens with a number of thematic threads, drawn from different modal segments, which bear on the character of the young American intellectual on the eve of America's entrance into the war.[8] The Camera Eye persona has had the shields protecting him from experience stripped away by his parents' deaths and his own partici-

---

7. Pizer's *Dos Passos' "U.S.A."* provides a full account of the relationship of the formal elements of the trilogy to cubism and to film montage.

8. The most useful studies of *Nineteen-Nineteen* are Barbara Foley's "History, Fiction, and Satirical Form: The Example of Dos Passos' *1919*," *Genre*, XII (1979), 357–78; and Lois Hughson's "Dos Passos's World War: Narrative Technique and History," *Studies in the Novel*, XII (1980), 46–61.

pation in the war. In particular, the "bellglass" of Harvard—the Harvard aestheticism of "Copey's beautiful reading voice," "handsomely bound books," and "artificial parmaviolet scent," all of which has constituted a death-in-life (or "ethercone," as Dos Passos remarks elsewhere)[9]—has been shattered by the violent physicality of war, not only of washing windows and cleaning spark plugs but of "grinding the American Beauty roses to dust in that whore's bed" and inhaling the "almond smell of high explosives." And with this breaking-out of the protective womb of family and college into life in all its crass vulgarity there might come, the Camera Eye anticipates, a new vision born of new experience: "tomorrow I hoped would be the first day of the first month of the first year."[10]

The biography of Jack Reed, which follows the opening Camera Eye, and the first narrative segment about Richard Savage make clear the divergent paths the young Harvard graduate can take as he emerges from his artificial world into one of conflict and testing. Jack Reed has also heard "Copey's voice reading" and the "dim voices in lecturehalls" (35). But once out in the world, he seeks to act on his belief that "words meant what they said" (37) and accordingly demands that the democratic ideals expressed in our sacred civil texts be made operative in social actuality. He has thus freed himself from the limitations of his class and background, represented above all by his Harvard education, and has become a fighter for social justice. He is the first of a large number of real-life figures biographically present in *Nineteen-Nineteen* who, along with the Camera Eye and Richard Savage, give concrete form to the crisis of intellect and spirit facing upper-class young men who enter a world shaped largely by the efforts of their class to perpetuate its power for its own self-interest. The writer Randolph Bourne and the diplomat Paxton Hibben, the first a graduate of Columbia and the second of Princeton, will share Reed's capacity to reject his class heritage and speak out for truth, especially in refusing to yield to the immense pressure to support the war. By contrast, two others of a similar—though somewhat earlier—eastern-university establishment background, Woodrow Wilson and Theodore Roosevelt, are captives of their class.

Dick Savage's temperament, which will unfold fully to define his

9. Dos Passos, *The 42nd Parallel* (1930; rpr. New York, 1969), "Camera Eye (25)," 311.
10. Dos Passos, *Nineteen-Nineteen* (1932; rpr. New York, 1969), 33–34. Further citations of this edition will appear in the text.

destiny during his Paris experience, is incipient in his youth, including his Harvard years. Insecure because of his father's absence and the tenuous financial position of his socially conscious mother, he early learns to capitalize on his good looks and facile tongue to get what he wants and evade difficulties. In late adolescence, for example, he not only ingratiates himself with a young cleric and his wife but readily adopts the language of religious faith to extenuate sleeping with the wife. "Physical things didn't matter and . . . repentance was the key of redemption," he tells a friend, and meanwhile he and the woman "went on sinning" (102). Harvard becomes possible for Savage through his cultivation of the wealthy Hiram Halsey Cooper, who shows "him first editions of Beardsley and Huysmans" (102)—a clearly coded allusion to Cooper's homosexual interest in the young man. At Harvard, after a freshman year in which he inadvertently lands among the "wrong people" (105)—Jews and social activists and graduate students—he is absorbed into the reigning aesthetic crowd, hears Copey read, and finds a close companion in Ned Wigglesworth. Both write poetry and "had tea and conversation about books and poets in the afternoon and lit the room with candles" (107).

Dos Passos establishes a significant sexual symbolism within the Harvard context of *Nineteen-Nineteen,* one which will become stronger during the part of the novel set in Paris. An unambiguously masculine Jack Reed rejects the homoerotic undercurrent of Harvard aestheticism and pushes courageously—and ultimately tragically—into the world, to struggle "manfully" for honesty and justice. Savage, however, though he has not yet revealed a homosexual inclination (this will come later), absorbs and reflects the lack of moral strength that Dos Passos associates with the homosexuality-tinged aestheticism of Harvard. That weakness is apparent in two incidents during Savage's final year at Harvard, incidents that, in turning on a willingness to betray friend and conviction, have almost exact counterparts later in Paris. Opposed to the conflict in Europe—as most of Harvard was before America entered the war— Dick writes an antiwar sonnet and submits it when a magazine runs a literary contest. "It won the prize, but the editors wrote back that they would prefer a note of hope in the last sestet. Dick put in the note of hope" (111). On the night of Wilson's reelection in November, 1916, when Dick and Ned go to Boston to celebrate, Ned gets drunk and picks up a sailor and a boxing instructor. Frightened, Dick deserts his friend and returns to Cambridge alone.[11] The Camera Eye persona,

11. Ned's homosexuality, more clearly defined at this point than Dick's, is revealed when he

therefore, as he emerges from the "ethercone" of Harvard, stands poised between the alternatives offered by Jack Reed and Richard Savage. He can opt for the masculine strength of truth telling and rebelliousness or he can lean toward a homosexuality-tainted weakness of will and spirit.

Both the Camera Eye and Dick encounter the war at first hand as members of American volunteer ambulance units in northern France and Italy. The two young men instinctively recognize the discrepancy between the carnage they are encountering and the rhetoric used to support the war. Temporarily relieved from frontline duty at Verdun, the Camera Eye sits in a deserted garden and remembers the "muddy scraps of flesh you put in the ambulance." He reflects, *"No   there must be some way"* (118) to preserve liberty, other than the obscene mix of meaningless deaths and of patriotic slogans and icons wheeled out to support them. *"Patrick Henry in khaki submits to short arm inspection* [for a venereal disease] *and puts all his pennies* [penises?] *in a Liberty Loan"* (119).

Dick, too, finds himself in the temporary refuge of the little garden at Récicourt. And he, too, has seen death and has heard the French soldiers saying that "la guerre was one saloperie" and crying, "A bas la guerre, mort aux vaches" (197). He and his comrades "talk about how they'd go back to the States and start an underground newspaper like *La Libre Belgique* to tell people what the war was really like" (199). As Dick's French ambulance group is disbanded and he joins a new Red Cross unit formed for service in Italy, his belief in the futility and moral corruption of the war is again and again confirmed. It is the "most gigantic cockeyed graft of the century" (201), one of his fellow volunteers exclaims. And Joe Williams tells him, from his perspective as a wartime merchant seaman, that "this whole goddam war's a gold brick, it ain't on the level, it's crooked from A to Z" (208). Deeply disturbed, Dick writes to old friends in the United States who support the war that when anyone urges young men "to go into this cockeyed lunatic asylum of war he's doing everything he can to undermine all the principles and ideals he most believes in" (210). The letter leads to Dick's dismissal from the ambulance service, and on his way home to America he decides on open rebellion. He will cross into Spain, where he can live freely and write antiwar poetry. "What people needed was stirring poems to nerve them for revolt against their cannibal governments" (219). For crossing the Pyrenees, he buys a compass.

---

tells Dick the following day that he ended up with the sailor and the boxer in a Turkish bath, a "most curious place" (110).

Although Dick's and the Camera Eye's rebellions appear alike—and the similarity is reinforced by the duplication of specific settings and events in their experiences at Verdun and in Italy—Dick's is suspect because of the adaptive and ingratiating role playing that is its context. All Dick's friends in the ambulance corps are against the war, and Dick is also spurred by the "daydream of himself living in a sun-scorched Spanish town, sending out flaming poems and manifestos, calling young men to revolt against their butchers" (219). No wonder he is easily deflected from his purpose when he meets his old Harvard friend Ned Wigglesworth on the train to Bordeaux. In Wigglesworth there is the symbol of the even more magnetic allure of Harvard apolitical aestheticism and morally untaxing self-indulgence. The two friends get drunk together, and Dick is soon on a ship back to the United States rather than tramping across the mountains to Spain. During the sea crossing, he discovers the compass in his jacket pocket. "Guiltily, he fished it out and dropped it overboard" (221).

The divergence between the Camera Eye and Richard Savage, which the similarity of their careers to mid-1918 obscures, is fully evident during the second phase of their European experiences. Dick lets himself be co-opted into support of the war and becomes an officer. By currying favor with several senior officers and trading on his family background—his mother's father was a general—he works his way into a comfortable berth as a courier stationed in Paris during the peace conference. The Camera Eye, on the other hand, must face the ordinary indignities of life as an enlisted man until he is assigned to the Sorbonne Detachment. The two figures are thus in very different social and moral positions when they settle down in Paris in the spring of 1919.

Like other expatriate writers, Dos Passos uses his characters' responsiveness to the richness of the Paris moment, and especially its capacity to stimulate the creative imagination, as a gauge for distinguishing between expatriates who are honest and courageous in their lives and art and those who are not. And like Hemingway in particular, he exploits an association of homosexuality with artistic and moral flabbiness as a symbolic indicator of that distinction.

The section labeled "Camera Eye (39)" is an impressive representation of Paris as a matrix of spiritual awakening. In its compressed yet intensely evocative dramatization of the impact of Paris on the alert heart and intelligence—of Paris both as a "Nouvelle Athènes" of artistic, literary, and musical activity and as a place physically rich and fulfilling, in the "warm bulge" of the servant girl's breasts, in the "smell

of chicory in coffee," and in the multicolored cityscape—the section
commands full quotation:

daylight enlarges out of ruddy quiet very faintly throbbing wanes into
my sweet darkness broadens red through the warm blood weighting the
lids warmsweetly then snaps on
    enormously blue yellow pink
    today is Paris   pink sunlight hazy on the clouds against patches of
robinsegg   a tiny siren hoots shrilly   traffic drowsily rumbles clat-
ters over the cobbles taxis squawk   the yellow's the comforter through
the open windows the Louvre emphasizes its sedate architecture of grey-
pink stone between the Seine and the sky
    and the certainty of Paris
    the towboat shiny green and red chugs against the current   towing
three black and mahoganyvarnished barges   their deckhouse windows have green shutters and lace curtains and pots of geraniums in
flower   to get under the bridge a fat man in blue had to let the little
black stack drop flat to the deck
    Paris comes into the room in the servantgirl's eyes the warm bulge
of her breasts under the grey smock   the smell of chicory in coffee
scalded milk and the shine that crunches on the crescent rolls stuck with
little dabs of very sweet unsalted butter
    in the yellow paperback of the book that halfhides the agreeable
countenance of my friend
    Paris of 1919
    paris-mutuel
    roulettewheel that spins round the Tour Eiffel red square white square
a million dollars a billion marks a trillion roubles baisse du franc or a
mandate for Montmartre
    Cirque Médrano the steeplechase gravity of cellos tuning up on the
stage at the Salle Gaveau oboes and a triangle   la musique s'en fou
de moi says the old marchioness jingling with diamonds as she walks
out on Stravinski   but the red colt took the jumps backwards and we
lost all our money
    la peinture opposite the Madeleine   Cézanne Picasso Modigliani
    Nouvelle Athènes
    la poesie of manifestos always freshtinted on the kiosks and slogans
scrawled in chalk on the urinals L'UNION DES TRAVAILLEURS
FERA LA PAIX DU MONDE
    revolution round the spinning Eiffel Tower

that burns up our last year's diagrams the dates fly off the calendar we'll make everything new today is the Year I   Today is the sunny morning of the first day of spring   We gulp our coffee splash water on us jump into our clothes run downstairs step out wideawake into the first morning of the first day of the first year (344–45)

The passage is controlled by its opening image of an awakening to the richness of life—the daylight initially warming the blood and then snapping on the "enormously blue yellow pink" of Paris "today," a Paris of pleasing street noises, river scenes, broad vistas, and a frank acceptance of the pleasures of food, drink, and sexuality. The Camera Eye is also awakening to a Paris of artistic innovation and of political excitement engendered by the peace conference—of gambling for mandates and of "la poesie of manifestos." Dos Passos wishes to communicate both the abundance and the vibrancy that the Paris moment has for the Camera Eye, who has been temporarily freed from not only the social and moral squalor but also the constraints of American life, both symbolized by his military service, and now finds himself in a world encouraging the expression of his deepest nature. No wonder, then, that the Paris moment for the Camera Eye is not only a sunny morning in spring but an Edenic rebirth of the spirit to a new life, "the first morning of the first day of the first year." The manner in which this closing line echoes that of the first Camera Eye of the novel—"tomorrow I hoped would be the first day of the first month of the first year" (34)—suggests that his earlier hope for a new and freer life to result from his liberation from parents and Harvard has indeed met with fulfillment in the Paris moment.

Dick Savage, on the other hand, functions within a very different Paris, especially in its sexual character. Even before he returns to the city in early 1919, the Paris of his narrative sections is that of an open sexuality cheapened and vulgarized by the tensions of war. Prostitutes engulf his ambulance unit on its arrival. "Fellows . . . this aint a war," one of his comrades exclaims. "It's a goddam whorehouse" (114). That sentiment is echoed by a Newsreel lyric:

> Oh that battle of Paree
> It's making a bum out of me
> Toujours la femme et combien (223)

Savage, on his return, brings to this world of bought sex the taint of his own covert purchase by his patron Horace Halsey Cooper, who has arranged his commission. Sharing a hotel suite in crowded Washington, Dick sleeps on the couch. "After he'd rolled up in the sheet, Dick heard Mr. Cooper tiptoe over and stand beside the couch breathing hard" (349).

The motifs of Dick's unacknowledged homosexuality yet of his exploitation of his homosexual attraction become even more explicit within the moral climate of the peace conference. One evening not long after his return, his colonel takes him to dine luxuriously at Voisin's, and later a conference participant lectures him on the importance of oil in determining political decisions at the conference. If soldiers in the trenches "thought the war was lousy," Dick's interlocutor comments, "wait till they see the peace. . . . Oh, boy, wait till they see the peace" (359). Dick walks home. "At the corner of the Boulevard Sébastopol a whitefaced young man who was walking the other way looked quickly into his face and stopped" (360).

It is within this context of hypocrisy and deception in both world politics and personal relations that Dick's seduction and subsequent desertion of Daughter—Anne Elizabeth Trent—are to be understood. A headstrong, ingenuous, and tomboyish young Texan, Daughter is Dos Passos' rough symbolic approximation of American innocence. When Dick meets her shortly after the evening at Voisin's, a "pink-cheeked girl" (362) with a Texas drawl, he finds himself drawn to her. The basis of the attraction becomes clear when, soon afterward, he dreams of a "young Texas boy with pink cheeks who wanted to . . ." (363; Dos Passos' ellipsis). Dos Passos' emphasis here on Dick's underlying sexual preference is less to express a Hemingwayesque visceral disgust—he had depicted homosexuality with some sympathy in earlier works— than to portray Dick's weak moral center in sexual terms.[12] Dick is guided by a powerful strain of self-interest that simultaneously exploits and suppresses his sexual nature. He will seduce Daughter for her tomboyish attractiveness but will have little compunction about discarding her when she becomes a hindrance in his career.

The differences between the Camera Eye and Dick within the Paris moment are, of course, established not only by the contrast between the Camera Eye's responsiveness to the "warm bulge" of the servant girl's breasts and Dick's return of a glance by a "whitefaced young man" on a lonely Paris street. The Camera Eye lives in a Paris of cheap hotels and restaurants in the Contrescarpe and similar quartiers, and his friends

12. See Dos Passos' sympathetic characterization of Tony Hunter in *Manhattan Transfer* (1925).

are other enlisted men with the Sorbonne Detachment and French workingmen. Dick, as an officer loosely attached to the peace conference, is soon absorbed into a very different world, one shaped by the upper-class roles and preoccupations of Eleanor and Eveline and by the wartime and peace-conference political maneuvering of J. Ward Moorehouse. Whereas the Paris of the Camera Eye is rendered with poetic compression, Dick's Paris is depicted in great detail, since he appears not only in his own narratives but in those of Eveline and Daughter.

Eleanor and Eveline arrive in Paris as Red Cross volunteers in late 1917, when the war is in full fury. In a satiric portrait of the American capacity to distance oneself through class from social chaos, they set up a version of a New York artistic salon in the most fashionable area of the Left Bank, in a "fine apartment" opposite Notre-Dame. "They had tea on a small Buhl table in the window almost every evening when they got home from the office on Rue de Rivoli, after spending the day pasting pictures of ruined French farms and orphaned children and starving warbabies into scrapbooks to be sent home for use in Red Cross drives" (225). They give dinner parties, Eveline has a series of minor affairs, and Eleanor collects antiques. When they visit the front, accompanied by Moorehouse, they are entertained in the officers' mess, "and all the young officers were so nice to them" (236).

With the end of the war, Moorehouse' prominent position in the peace conference raises the level of Eleanor's and Eveline's social life to that of the Ritz Bar, the Opera, and Montmartre nightclubs. (Moorehouse and Eleanor have secretly been lovers for some years.) If Paris is the "capital of the world" during the peace conference, its capitol is the Hôtel Crillon, where the American delegation has its headquarters and Moorehouse has a suite that Dick, Eleanor, and Eveline often visit. Dick is now very much a part of this world. Earlier, during his rebellious phase, his Paris had been that of the Pantheon working-class quartier. But it has become the Crillon and "trips to Brussels on the night express, lobster cardinal washed down with Beaune on the red plush settees at Larue's, champagne cocktails at the Ritz Bar, talks full of the lowdown over a demie at the Café Weber" (356).

The moral texture of Dick's current Paris is evident, however, not only in the obvious signposts of overindulgence but also in the deception and betrayal implicit in the sexual lives of the group of which he has become part. Eveline casually sleeps with a number of men, but then invites an affair with Moorehouse after he explains to her his relationship with Eleanor—"how people had misunderstood their

The dining room of the Hôtel Crillon

beautiful friendship that had always been free from the sensual and degrading" (314). Shortly afterward she finds Eleanor and Moorehouse in bed and turns to Paul Johnson, a shy and nondescript enlisted man, who makes her pregnant.

If Eveline resembles Daughter in the ease with which men victimize her, Eleanor is similar to Moorehouse in the calculating efficiency of her manipulation of all aspects of her personal relationships, including the sexual, for her own advantage. (Both she and Moorehouse use sex as they use language: to persuade and deceive.) Thus, once Daughter is on the scene, an Eleanor-Dick-Daughter triangle centering on a battle for Dick's soul quickly develops. Daughter is responsive to the vestiges of the artist in Dick—"You're my poet, Dick" (374), she tells him the first time she sleeps with him—while Eleanor seeks to enlist Dick as one of Moorehouse' "bright young men" (383) in his public relations firm. The struggle reaches a crisis when Daughter becomes pregnant. Confronted by Eleanor's counsel that "an unsuitable marriage has been the ruination of many a promising young fellow" (389) and by Daughter's pleas for his aid, he acquiesces in the direction his life has taken since he has returned to Paris and seeks to dissuade Daughter from pressing any claim against him. Their climactic scene together, in Dick's hotel room near the Gare Saint-Lazare, finds Dick acting out the role not of a poet attuned to human needs and emotions but of a public-relations expert relentlessly persuading by any means and at whatever cost to personal integrity. He has already recently played this role in freeing his brother, who is also in Paris, from the demands of a French girl he made pregnant, and he now tries to do the same for himself with Daughter. In the face of her hopeful expectation that he will make things right—she loves him and has faith in him—he explains the damaging effect a marriage would have on his career and then skillfully shifts onto her the responsibility for extricating herself from her difficulty. "If you want to get married," he tells her, "there are plenty of fellows who'd give their eyeteeth to marry you" (391). When she resists this ploy, he exclaims, "It's no more my fault than it is yours . . . if you'd taken proper precautions" (392).

Daughter at last can no longer hide from herself Dick's essential weakness and the hopelessness of her appeal to his conscience and rushes out. Dick, alone in his hotel room, is at first miserable. He listens to the late-night street noise outside his room—taxicabs honking, café shutters coming down—and also pictures the prostitutes roaming the streets. His bed is cold and clammy, but as it gets warmer, he gradually dismisses thoughts of Daughter and of the strident and shabby Paris street world reflecting his own moral state and thinks of the day to come—how dressed in his officer's uniform he will spend a meaningless day followed by late afternoon tea at Eleanor's, where he will learn more about his job with Moorehouse. And he falls asleep.

By the conclusion of the Paris spring of 1919, the Camera Eye and Dick have fully revealed their contrary reactions to the Paris moment—the one stimulated to a responsiveness to the possibilities of life and art, the other exposing his underlying weakness of spirit. They are both, however, only at a middle stage in the full unleashing of these states of mind. The Camera Eye's readiness to reject his middle-class origins is undercut by the almost comic failure of the May 1st revolutionary uprising in Paris and by the channeling of radical ideology into middle-class forms, as in the Anarchists' picnic he attends. The final Camera Eye of *Nineteen-Nineteen* finds him once again enmeshed by his coercive American background: he is mechanically loading and unloading scrap iron from a railroad car while waiting to recover his lost identity papers so that the army can discharge him. He has discovered in Paris the kind of life he wishes to lead in America—that of a free engagement with the richness of life—but he has yet to discover how to achieve such engagement within his American identity and his American conditions of life.

Dick, on the other hand, has seemingly found his way. In one of the last scenes in which we encounter him before his discharge from the army, he appears at a luxurious restaurant accompanied by Moore-house and Eleanor and is distant and formal toward Daughter when they meet accidentally. On his discharge, Dick does indeed begin work-ing in Paris for Moorehouse, who has landed the Standard Oil public-relations account. Our last view of him in *Nineteen-Nineteen* is at a dreary farewell party for the pregnant Eveline, which he attends after participating in a news conference where Moorehouse has proclaimed a "new era of international co-operation . . . dawning in which great aggregations of capital would work together for peace and democracy" (458). It is not out of harmony with Dick's capitulation to the ethic of personal and political duplicity that marks this concluding scene—of Eveline's and Daughter's sexual victimization and of Moorehouse' ma-nipulation of the language of democratic idealism—that he is viciously baited by one of Eveline's radical friends, who goes on to call him a "goddam fairy" (460).

Dick has gotten what he wanted out of his Paris moment: a rich life-style, a love affair without serious consequences to himself, and a good job. He has done so, however, at the price of having his dishonesty constantly and painfully made apparent to himself. The Camera Eye faces a future that is problematical, given his need to translate his newfound sense of himself into the specifics of life in America, but Dick can look forward only to the dead end of a tormenting recognition of his self-betrayal. By associating Dick's "selling out" of his potential as a poet with his participation in Moorehouse' corrupt manipulation of the language of political idealism, Dos Passos connects Dick's moral collapse to the larger American betrayal of the nation's heritage of democratic idealism during the war and at the peace conference. The stage is thus set for the full working out in *The Big Money* of the states of mind and spirit crystallized in the Camera Eye and Dick by their participation in the Paris moment. The Camera Eye will devote himself to proclaiming America's betrayal of its heritage of "old words," and Dick will degenerate into Moorehouse' surrogate in the morally corrupt New York advertising world.

F. Scott Fitzgerald
Tender Is the Night

Unlike Stein, Hemingway, Nin, and Miller, Fitzgerald was not a resident of Paris for an extended period. His years of European travel, from 1921 to 1931, were those of his greatest popularity as a short-story writer. Not for him, therefore, the typical expatriate life of a small Left Bank apartment or shabby hotel. He and his family lived and traveled in considerable style—as Hemingway noted with some contempt in *A Moveable Feast*—more in the manner of a well-to-do tourist than a self-exiled artist. Nevertheless, Fitzgerald was soaking up an expatriate ambience, though of a distinctive kind. It is possible to trace the principal settings of *Tender Is the Night* in the Fitzgeralds' European travels of 1925–1931: the stay in Paris during the spring of 1925, the visit to Sara and Gerald Murphy's Villa America, at Antibes, that summer and to the Somme battlefield that fall, a riotous period in Paris during the summer of 1928, a further visit to the Riviera in the in summer of 1929, and lengthy stays in Switzerland after Zelda Fitzgerald's breakdown in early 1930.[1]

After the poor reception of *Tender Is the Night* in 1934, Fitzgerald decided that his unusual device of opening the novel in midplot and then returning to the earlier lives of his protagonists had puzzled and

1. For a chronology of Fitzgerald's European travels of 1921–1931, see Matthew J. Bruccoli, *Some Sort of Epic Grandeur: The Life of F. Scott Fitzgerald* (New York, 1981). Bruccoli also identifies the biographical sources for the fictional characters and events of *Tender Is the Night*. André Le Vot ("Fitzgerald in Paris," *Fitzgerald-Hemingway Annual, 1973*, 49–63) estimates that between 1921 and 1931 Fitzgerald was abroad four and a half years, of which he spent three in France and twenty-two months in Paris.

disconcerted many readers. He therefore projected and partly prepared a version of the novel, published posthumously in 1951, in which the action occurs in a single forward-moving march of events. The burden of almost all critical commentary on Fitzgerald that bears on the relative merits of the two versions has been that the *in medias res* narrative form of 1934 is superior to the single chronology of 1951. Since I share this view, for reasons that will become clear, I have made the original 1934 version the basis for my discussion of the work.[2]

Tender Is the Night is in part a recapitulation and reconceptualization of Henry James's international theme. In Fitzgerald's novel, as in several of James's greatest works, an American innocent interacts with a more sophisticated and morally suspect European culture and suffers a tragic fall. As we come to know Dick Diver in *Tender Is the Night,* we realize that beneath his surface charm, poise, and control lies a reservoir of naïve and impulsive idealism, a faith in the human enterprise which Fitzgerald roots firmly in the American experience and character. Dick arrives in Zurich in 1917 as a young man harboring the "illusions of eternal strength and health, and of the essential goodness of people; illusions of a nation, the lies of generations of frontier mothers who had to croon falsely that there were no wolves outside the cabin door."[3] Dick's father, a gentle but firm-minded clergyman, has instilled in him a chivalric corollary of this affirmative view of human nature—that "nothing could be superior to 'good instincts,' honor, courtesy, and courage" (204). Dick's conscious code of role and duty, of a commitment to help others, has, however, an unconscious but powerful complement in his need to have his worth as an exponent of the code recognized and valued. As Fitzgerald sums up Dick's character at the close of the novel, his desire to behave with chivalric rectitude, to make operative in life both his sense of duty and the appraisal of his personal worth that this quality of mind would properly elicit, has resulted in his having "chosen the sweet poison and drunk it. Wanting above all to be brave and kind, he had wanted, even more than that, to be loved" (300).

The setting for Dick's fulfilment of the tragic potential of his inno-

2. Milton R. Stern ("*Tender Is the Night:* The Text Itself," in *Critical Essays on F. Scott Fitzgerald's "Tender Is the Night,"* ed. Milton R. Stern [Boston, 1986], 21–31) provides a history and overview of the issue. Stern himself believes that the 1951 version should receive more critical attention than it does.

3. *Tender Is the Night* (1934; rpr. New York, 1981), 115–16. Further citations of this edition will appear in the text.

cence—innocence about both the world in general and his own needs and nature in particular—is a European civilization that has already passed from illusion to disbelief and cynicism. Dick realizes the geographical and historical distance between the world of faith that produced his own codes and values and a Europe emptied of traditional value when he visits a striking reminder for his generation of the collapse of the old order, the trenches of northern France. The Battle of the Somme, Dick cries, "took religion and years of plenty and tremendous sureties. . . . You had to have a whole-souled sentimental equipment going back further than you could remember" (56). But though Dick can exclaim that "all my beautiful lovely safe world blew itself up here" (57), he also ruefully acknowledges that he remains an "old romantic" (57)—that unlike the deeply wounded Jake Barnes, he has preserved intact into the present the beliefs and values of his native origin and past.

James in his international novels often renders the distinction between American innocence and European experience by depicting recently arrived Americans who encounter European civilization in the form of Europeanized Americans and deeply foreboding settings. *Portrait of a Lady* offers a useful example in the figures of Gilbert Osmond and Madame de Merle and in Osmond's Florence and Rome palazzos. To a degree, the same encounter occurs in *Tender Is the Night,* especially in Dick's acquaintance with the Warren family, of Chicago, whose great wealth and power are absorbed into European life and then play a destructive role in the determination of Dick's fate, and in the Somme battlefield. But even more than James, and especially the late James, in whose work the details of place are often indirectly rendered, Fitzgerald in *Tender Is the Night* deploys the particulars of setting—and especially those of Paris—to constitute the crucible in which innocence is tested and found inadequate as a guide to survival in the modern world. Antibes and Paris and Rome will, by their distinctive qualities, precipitate the emergence and shape the expression of Dick's essential character.

Fitzgerald divides *Tender Is the Night* into three books. The first, set in Antibes and Paris in the summer of 1925, concentrates on the mutual infatuation of Dick and Rosemary Hoyt. The second takes us back to Dick's arrival in Europe in 1917, his marriage to Nicole Warren in 1919, and, briefly, their life together until the summer of 1925. This book then returns to the present of the Divers shortly after their visit to Paris in 1925 and continues with their lives until Dick's beating by the Rome police in late 1928. The third book, the shortest, deals with Dick's decline in Switzerland and Antibes until his break with Nicole and his departure from Europe in the summer of 1929.[4] The tripartite chronological format serves a number of obvious purposes. We are introduced to Dick in Book One at a pivotal moment in his life. Book Two relates the origin and consequences of the moment, and Book Three its sequel. But the tripartite format, focusing as it does on time periods, tends to obscure the importance of place in the thematics of the novel, especially of Antibes and Paris early in the work and Rome and Antibes at its close.[5] Put briefly, each place provides the reader, in an increasing degree of revelation, with the context for what can be called a negative epiphany—that is, a sudden realization, prompted by a climactic scene at the conclusion of the narrative set in that place, of Dick's tragic condition and impending fate.

It is during the six days that Dick, Nicole, Rosemary, and the Norths spend in Paris, shortly after the opening of the novel in Antibes, that the basic configuration of Dick's character shows forth. Paris is thus, in its various sites, activities, and figures, a catalyst for exposing what was disguised in Antibes and what will receive a fuller disclosure in the remainder of the novel. It is for this reason that Fitzgerald's initial plan for *Tender Is the Night,* which highlights the Paris section by making it the climax of our introduction to Dick and his world, is superior to the revision, in which the Paris section comes after we are fully aware of Dick's and Nicole's early lives. What is arresting revelation in the novel as it originally appeared is almost anticlimactic in the later version.

Another formal aspect of *Tender Is the Night,* its selection of points of view, is—like its exploitation of place—independent of the division of the novel into three books. The selection of points of view has a decisive impact on the opening sections set in Antibes and Paris. We encounter Dick and his group at Antibes through Rosemary, whose

4. As has been pointed out by, among others, Matthew Bruccoli ("Material for a Centenary Edition of *Tender Is the Night,*" in *Critical Essays,* ed. Stern, 33–34), Fitzgerald's chronology is awry in Books Two and Three of *Tender Is the Night:* though he mentions that five years have elapsed between the summer of 1925 and the conclusion of the novel, he also places the conclusion in the summer of 1929.

5. The similarity I noted earlier between *Portrait of a Lady* and *Tender Is the Night* can be extended to the device in both novels of rendering theme through the symbolic implications of a sequence of places—Gardencourt, Florence, Rome, and (briefly again) Gardencourt in *Portrait of a Lady*—that maps the protagonist's decline from a fullness of energy and spirit to an acknowledgment of failure.

point of view Fitzgerald maintains, except for one brief interruption, throughout the Antibes section. In Paris, Rosemary at first continues to be allotted the point of view, but Fitzgerald gradually transfers it, as though to indicate a broader base of understanding, to Dick, Nicole, and even Abe North. Dick's point of view is the prevailing one in Books Two and Three, except for the final portion of the novel, when in the return to Antibes, with Dick defeated and disheartened, Nicole's takes over. Just as Fitzgerald's sense of an apt fictional dynamics led him to discard a sequential chronology for an opening *in medias res,* so it made him realize that what is at first appearance an unstable point of view could give us a better understanding of Dick's fall from the height of apparent power and grace, where Rosemary perceived him to stand at Antibes, to the low of a "ruined" (264) life, in Nicole's final estimation, again at Antibes.

Rosemary's youthful impressionability lends an aura of the magical to the Divers at Antibes.[6] On the almost deserted beach of a former winter resort, Dick is for Rosemary a kind of Prospero who, outside space and time, looks after the well-being of his subjects with style and aplomb. (Dick carefully raking the beach for stones is a half-facetious allusion to this role.) Rosemary, as a very young but very successful movie actress, is conditioned to respond immediately and boldly to experience, in the way young girls do in her films. Moreover, her greatest triumph, we later learn, has been in the film *Daddy's Girl,* in which her devotion to her father drives the plot. It is not surprising, then, that when she encounters Dick, Nicole, and Abe and Mary North on the beach, she is quickly attracted by Dick's poise and his mastery over the group. When he invites her to join them, he seems "kind and charming—his voice promised that he would take care of her, and that a little later he would open up whole new worlds for her, unroll an endless succession of magnificent possibilities" (15).

The brave new world that awaits her, however, has its Caliban in the several gauche Americans who occupy another part of the beach and wish to absorb her into their circle. The McKiscos (he a blocked but self-important writer, she bitchy and censorious), Mrs. Abrams (a decayed hanger-on), and Mr. Dumphry and Mr. Campion (fatuous homosexuals) constitute a version of the American expatriate community

---

6. A good deal of the best criticism of *Tender Is the Night* is collected in *Tender Is the Night: Essays in Criticism,* ed. Marvin J. LaHood (Bloomington, Ind., 1970), and in *Critical Essays,* ed. Stern. In addition, see John B. Chambers, *The Novels of F. Scott Fitzgerald* (New York, 1989).

of thin art and dry sexuality that Hemingway satirized in *The Sun Also Rises* and *A Moveable Feast*. Dick's magic, however, saves Rosemary from the McKiscos, for she accepts his invitation and joins his group, and it is also effective at the dinner party at the Divers' Villa Diana to which she is invited. There, the controlling image for the aura of romance and power that Dick radiates shifts somewhat from Prospero to a movie director. The reader by now knows of the significance that films have for Rosemary: Fitzgerald has mentioned her career and her visit to a nearby studio, and the film director Brady is present at the dinner party. So, on the romantic set of the garden of a Riviera villa in the early evening, a varied cast gathers and interacts. There is some early discord, since Dick has invited the McKisco crowd and the two groups do not mix well, but soon Dick's and Nicole's attention to their guests brings about a transformation and "they were only their best selves" (31) as the "Divers began suddenly to warm and glow and expand, as if to make up to their guests, already so subtly assured of their importance" (33).

After these encounters, the Divers—and especially Dick—indeed possess a kind of "magic" (33) for Rosemary, and her response is to fall in love with Dick. But if Rosemary were less of a romantic seeking romance, she might notice much in the life of the Divers that clashes with her dream that she can act out an idealized instance of herself as Daddy's girl with Dick as her father and lover. We ourselves have caught several hints of the limits of her understanding of Dick and his world. In the one brief scene that is not narrated from her point of view, Dick tells Nicole that he plans to invite the McKisco crowd to the dinner party notwithstanding his evident distaste for them. "I want to give a really *bad* party," he says to Nicole. This is out of character for the Dick we have met through Rosemary, the Dick whose knack is to anticipate and defuse difficulties. "I want to give a party where there's a brawl and seductions and people going home with their feelings hurt and women passed out in the cabinet de toilette" (26). Given this intimation of the destructive self-hate in Dick's makeup—of his desire to seek the unpleasant in order to introduce pain into his life—we, unlike Rosemary, might decide to be more attentive to other signs of tension, discord, and failure in Dick and his group. Those would include Tommy Barban's only partly repressed desire for Nicole, Abe North's botched career as a composer, and above all, Dick's desire to please and charm Rosemary, Rosemary's susceptibility to his effort, and Nicole's extreme passivity, almost to the point of seeming drugged.

To Rosemary, however, and to a large extent the reader as well on first reading, the climactic scene of the dinner party is unexpected and inexplicable. Nicole and Dick are temporarily absent, and Mrs. McKisco returns from a trip to the bathroom with the announcement that "upstairs I came upon a scene, my dears—" (35). Rosemary is of course bewildered by the intrusion into the magical world of the Divers of moral turmoil that a viewer is at a loss for words to describe. Stripped of Rosemary's blurring vision, however, and in the context of the novel as a whole, the scene in the bathroom at the Villa Diana is the first of the negative epiphanies I referred to earlier. Dick's reaching out to charm and rescue Rosemary has aroused Nicole's jealous possessiveness and activated her principal stratagem for maintaining control over Dick, her irrationality. She has been having a hysterical outburst in the bathroom, Dick has been trying to calm her, and it is this scene—we come to learn later—that Mrs. McKisco stumbled upon.

But because we have been experiencing the Divers almost entirely through Rosemary's glowing and breathless reaction, because the scene in the bathroom is not described and its implications not made clear, we are not yet aware of the full import of what has been revealed. Leaving the party, Barban and McKisco quarrel about what Mrs. McKisco saw—Barban is aggressively protective of Nicole, McKisco is a fool—and a duel ensues in which there is much consumption of liquor but no injuries. (The film imagery is sustained in Mr. Dumphry's bringing a movie camera to record the duel.) But though all seems resolved with no harm done and considerable humor generated by McKisco's fear in the face of Tommy's "barbarism," the duel closes the first section of the novel on an ominous note. The discord in the Divers' life can permeate the world around them and cause disruption there as well as in their own lives.

Much that was beneath the surface at Antibes and that Rosemary either did not discern or did not comprehend—the tensions in Dick's overplayed role of gracious monarch of the island and Nicole's of passive subject, the various marks of failure and discord among the other members of Dick's group, and her own tendency toward the transforming of life into romantic film—comes into plain view and disastrously affects the lives of the principal characters in the section of the novel set in Paris which immediately follows the Divers' dinner party.

Since, as in much of Fitzgerald's fiction, chronology is frequently obscure during this section of the novel, it may be worth clarifying the sequence of events during the six days the Divers, Rosemary, and the

Norths spend in the city. When we join the group at lunch in a fashionable Right Bank restaurant, they are in the second day of their visit to Paris. They attended a dance the night before, and all has gone well so far: Dick and Nicole arrange to meet at their hotel later that afternoon to make love, and in the meantime she and Rosemary go shopping. The third day begins with a group excursion to the Somme battlefield. After dinner in Paris that evening, Rosemary attempts to interest Dick in an affair. The fourth day begins with more shopping. Later the group views Rosemary's film *Daddy's Girl* at a film studio, Dick and Rosemary attend a lesbian tea party, and the group goes on a wild romp through Paris that ends only at dawn. The fifth day begins with the group seeing Abe North off at the Gare Saint-Lazare, where an American woman shoots her departing lover, an Englishman. Dick spends the remainder of the day in increasingly frenetic attempts to be with Rosemary. The sixth and last day begins with the mystery of Abe's reappearance in Paris and his involvement in a serious case of misidentification of a purported thief. It concludes with the murder of the black man Peterson in Rosemary's hotel room and Nicole's subsequent collapse in her hotel bathroom.

Fitzgerald orchestrates the events of the last five days of the six-day visit—he records the activities of the first day only briefly and in retrospect—to culminate in the personal disorder manifest in Nicole's hysteria in her hotel bathroom. The settings for these events—almost all in the Right Bank world of well-to-do American visitors to the city—are deployed with incremental repetition to reveal the underlying flaws of the group and especially of Dick. Thus, Dick does his best to deflect Rosemary's aggressive overtures during their first taxi ride together, on the third day, but by the fourth day he is himself the eager lover in a cab. (Hotel rooms and bars, fashionable shops, and restaurants recur similarly, as we shall see.) In addition, the very events of the five days increasingly mirror the discord, emptiness, and violence implicit in the lives of the Divers and the Norths. When we first encounter the group, all is on the civilized level of a successful lunch, a husband desiring sex with his responsive wife, and a shopping tour. But after the visit to the trenches introduces the theme of the moral and physical chaos of modern life, the group's activities cant toward the opportunities for the bizarre, the tempestuous, and the violent that Paris offers. A lesbian tea party on the fourth day is followed by a "wild party" (79) that night, by the shooting of a negligent lover, and by the murder of an innocent black man. Here, too, there is increment, in that the increasingly extreme behavior of the group and of those around it chart the emergence into the open of the discord beneath the surface of the lives of Dick and his friends. And finally, Fitzgerald changes the narrative point of view from Rosemary to others as her cloudy understanding loses pertinence, given what the events themselves show us. Midway through the five days recounted, the viewpoint shifts to Dick, Abe North, and even Nicole, and it remains with them for the rest of the visit in order to display more openly and authoritatively the malaise present in each member of the group. (Rosemary and Dick share the point of view in the final hotel scenes of the section, however, since it is important there to record Rosemary's response to what she has come to realize about Dick and Nicole.)

In the Right Bank restaurant where we first see the group during the visit to Paris, Dick is amusingly in charge, and Rosemary is still the admiring point of view. As Fitzgerald remarks, "They had been two days in Paris but actually they were still under the beach umbrella" (51). Yet, several currents of feeling not present at the beach are in play beneath the genial surface of the occasion. Nicole's jealousy has been aroused by Rosemary, and Dick has gone out of his way to invite Rosemary to accompany the group to Paris (37)—this after the bathroom incident, as though he were challenging Nicole. And the restaurant is not really similar in tone and ambience to the sun-flushed beach with children playing in the sand and its air of permanent innocence. It is pervaded, with its "dark, smoky" atmosphere and its redolence of "rich raw foods on the buffet" (52), by the sensual, a quality confirmed almost immediately, when Rosemary overhears Dick and Nicole near the cloakroom. Dick asks, "—So you love me?" To Nicole's reply, "Oh, *do* I!" Dick says, "I want you terribly," and they arrange to meet at their hotel later that afternoon (53).

Rosemary, who had believed that Dick and Nicole were much "cooler" (53) in their relationship, is stunned by the revelation of a powerful and demanding sexuality. But here, as earlier, she has missed the underlying character of the exchange—in this case, especially the meaning of the "passionate gratitude" (53) in Nicole's "Oh, *do* I!" Dick does not desire Nicole merely because her handsome presence in a setting of rich food and wine has excited him sexually. He is also seeking to reassure her by his desire that he is still her lover and protector. Hence her "passionate gratitude." And he is also, perhaps now unconsciously, attempting to disarm her suspicion of his interest in Rosemary, an interest he has not yet acknowledged to himself.

Rosemary and Nicole go shopping that afternoon before Nicole is to meet Dick at the hotel. Here, too, there are intimations of a greater complexity and potential for discord in the lives of the Divers and of their charming guest than the image of the lord of the beach and the visiting princess accommodates. Nicole, it transpires, is extremely rich and hence possesses the power to control lives which wealth provides. And Rosemary, as Nicole leaves for her assignation with Dick, feels a pang of jealousy herself. "It was more difficult than she thought and her whole self protested as Nicole drove away" (55).

The next day the entire group undertakes an excursion common among Americans visiting Paris during the postwar years—a trip to the trenches of the Battle of the Somme. Once more there is a semblance of Antibes. Dick organizes the outing with the care he brings to the preparation of his parties, and Abe North plays the genial buffoon. But the trenches where only nine years earlier tens of thousands of men died meaninglessly because of a betrayed faith in their culture and its values has a powerful thematic reverberation for the remainder of the Paris visit. Faith and belief and an acceptance of the codes and forms of society have been destroyed by the very struggle to preserve them and have been replaced by the empty and trivial amusements of those who have survived—amusements typified by Abe's antics at the trenches and the doings of the group in Paris. Moreover, the battle scene and the lost values it signifies constitute a model of the current cultural moment in which violence without belief is the norm. Dick, as an "old romantic" (57), is instinctively aware of the implications of this model for him—that he is an anachronism of gentlemanly honor and duty who is being swept into the modern code of violently taking what one wants—and hence the somewhat hysterical tone of his posturing explanation to Rosemary of the meaning of the war. He himself was not at the Battle of the Somme but is to become a casualty.

Back in Paris that evening, Rosemary's impression of Dick's world is further tarnished when for the first time it registers with her that Abe North is in an almost permanent state of drunkenness. Rosemary's wish to please, to make herself desirable to Dick, induces her to conform to the ethos of the group as she is beginning to understand it. At dinner she takes her first drink, and in a taxi ride afterward she forces herself upon Dick. Dick, however, continues to presume her essential innocence, convinced that she is playacting a sexual involvement with him. "Such a lovely child," he says (62), as he resists her advances. Yet the phrase of distancing also expresses the basis of his deep attraction for Rosemary, inasmuch as her youth and innocence seek his protection and pay homage to his greater strength and wisdom. (There is in these scenes of Dick's and Rosemary's futile and undischarged longing in taxis an echo of Jake's and Brett's sexual frustration in their long taxi ride from Contrescarpe to Montparnasse early in *The Sun Also Rises*.) At their hotel, Rosemary persuades Dick to accompany her to her room and there invites him to "take" her (64). She "knew . . . that it was one of her greatest rôles and she flung herself into it . . . passionately" (64). But Dick, acting out his own role of gentleman protector, is unwilling and again refers to Rosemary as a "child" (65).

The Oedipal foundation of the attraction between Rosemary and Dick is painfully clear—especially, of course, to Dick himself, the professional psychiatrist—when the group gathers the following afternoon to view Rosemary's film *Daddy's Girl*. (Earlier in the day, Nicole and Rosemary have again gone shopping, with Rosemary increasingly jealous of Nicole.) The film cheapens and vulgarizes some of the principal values that have been lost in the modern world but which that world still clings to in sentimental nostalgia—above all those allied with a belief in the power of innocence and good to vanquish evil, or as is expressed through the character Rosemary plays in the film, the belief that in the face of her "fineness of character, her courage, her steadfastness" (69), the "forces of lust and corruption rolled away" (68). Although Dick recognizes the "vicious sentimentality" (69) of *Daddy's Girl,* the film, taken in conjunction with the visit to the trenches, is an almost exact symbolic equivalent of his own place in western ethical history. Whatever was true and honest in the human capacity to believe was lost on battlefields like the Somme, all that remains is the trivialization of that capacity in films like *Daddy's Girl,* and Dick, because he is seeking to maintain in his life the values of the civilization lost at the Somme, is himself acting out the vulgarization of the values the film debases. He is indeed doing so not only in general terms but explicitly in his mimicry of the sterile and destructive Oedipal fixations depicted in the film. And as though to ensure that we do not miss the point that Dick, whatever the nobility of his initial resistance to Rosemary's pursuit of him, is being absorbed into the banality of the film, Rosemary after the showing tries to persuade him to take a film test, since it's her dim plan that he should come to Hollywood and be her leading man.

After the film, when Dick and Rosemary are again together in a taxi, they conspire to drop off Collis Clay—a Yale undergraduate who is attempting to attach himself to Rosemary—and then kiss furtively on the way to a tea on the Left Bank.[7] Dick knows it is a lesbian party, but Rosemary does not until a "neat, slick girl with a lovely boy's face" (72) insistently tries to pick her up.[8] With these three scenes occurring in swift succession—the showing of *Daddy's Girl*, the taxi ride, and the lesbian tea party—there is a sharp drop in the sexual self-control of Dick's world. What had at least the appearance of restraint and courage the evening before is compromised by the self-indulgent Oedipal sexuality of the film, the furtive kissing in a cab, and the aggressive lesbianism of the tea. It is no wonder that when Dick and Rosemary leave the tea party and are alone in a cab for the third time, they are "lovers now" (73). They "lurched together. . . . Her breasts crushed flat against him, her mouth was all new and warm, owned in common" (74).

Of course, in this first physical release of their love, they still have "brave illusions about each other" and an "extraordinary innocence" (74) about their deepest motives. Another illusion for Dick, arising out of the innocence of his faith in his own strength and courage, is that he can somehow love Rosemary, while not consummating their love, and at the same time protect Nicole by disguising his love for the younger woman. Dick—as will become altogether plain when we learn the full story of his "saving" Nicole—is seeking to play out the part of heroic protector, and hence lover, of both women, an action comparable at the personal level to a civilization's acting out its heroic innocence and consequent moral chaos at the Battle of the Somme.

But for Dick chaos is still in the wings. That night he reprises his roles as master of the island and film director as he stage-manages a farewell party, one that has all of Paris as its setting, for Abe North, who is returning to America to try to resume his career as a composer. Once during the long night of the party, in a scene whose cloakroom setting ironically echoes Rosemary's earlier overhearing of Dick and Nicole, Rosemary's "damp powdery young body came up close to him in a crush of tired cloth, and stayed there, crushed against a background of other people's hats and wraps" (77).

The next day, the fifth and penultimate day of the Paris visit, begins with the group seeing Abe off at the Gare Saint-Lazare. Abe is the

7. Fitzgerald does not describe their embrace but rather writes of Rosemary's smoothing the "expressive disarray of her hair" (70) as they leave the cab.

8. Although Fitzgerald places the party on the rue Monsieur, in the Invalides section of Paris, and notes that the hostess is young, he otherwise appears to be alluding to Natalie Barney's Friday afternoon salon in her home on the rue Jacob. The woman who attempts to pick up Rosemary resembles Romaine Brooks, Barney's longtime companion, as portraits show her.

measure of the distance the group has come, or rather the extent to which it has revealed itself since the magic of Antibes, in that after days of heavy drinking he is "scarcely recognizable as the man who had swum upon Gausse's beach" (79). Nicole and Abe arrive at the station first (the first major shift from Rosemary's point of view), and in their conversation we learn of Abe's tormented love of many years' standing for Nicole, a love that has left him "heavy, belly-frightened" (81). The revelation of his agony is one more fissure in the image of the insouciant world of Antibes. Abe in his present condition—with his futile love for Nicole, his desperate fear that he has wasted his talent and career, and his compulsive drinking—both suggests the malaise at the heart of each member of the Divers' group and anticipates the almost precisely similar configuration of inner rot that is to become apparent in Dick.

Dick at this point, though, as on the previous evening, still seems very comfortably in charge, and his arrival at the station brings to the group a "fine glowing surface" (82). The glow is almost immediately extinguished, however, when an American woman, a Maria Wallis, shoots her departing English lover. The incident, though it does not directly involve the Divers, has resonance for their situation, since it underlines the violence and destruction latent in the circumstances of a spurned woman (read Nicole) and her unfaithful lover (read Dick). As the group leaves the station, Fitzgerald announces with heavy foreboding that "the shots had entered into all their lives; echoes of violence following them out onto the pavement" (85).

The state of fully accepting one's desire and thus its possible violent consequences, which the Saint-Lazare shooting represents, is one that Dick now rapidly assumes as he at last sheds the remnants of his seeming self-control. Collis Clay meets Dick in a restaurant and tells him a story of Rosemary's necking seriously with another Yale student on a train to Chicago the previous winter. The story may or may not be true— we ourselves do not know—but Dick believes it and becomes as anxious about Rosemary as any lover who has suddenly acquired a reason to doubt the innocence of his loved one. Rosemary has left for a meeting at her studio, and Dick is transformed into the tormented and pursuing lover. He follows her to the studio, not with any specific purpose in mind but "driven as an animal" despite his realization that "what he was now doing marked a turning point in his life" (91). Almost at this precise moment, Rosemary, having returned to her hotel room earlier than she expected, is writing to her mother about meeting a director at the studio: "I only saw him for a little while but I thought he was wonderful looking. I fell in love with him (Of course I Do Love Dick Best but you know what I mean)" (94). Thus, by the evening prior to their last day in Paris, Dick and Rosemary have been stripped of any possibility of sustaining the roles that the magic of Antibes generated and that Rosemary's point of view validated. Dick is no longer a Prospero looking after the well-being of his subjects with poise and grace but a Caliban in headlong pursuit of his desire. And Rosemary has been reduced from a fairy princess of transcendent purity and innocence to an adolescent whose infatuations have the capacity to create confusion and disorder.

The last day of the Paris section of *Tender Is the Night* begins ominously with a policeman looking for Abe North. His drunken irresponsibility has reached a culmination: as is shortly revealed, he returned to Paris after getting off the boat train before it reached Cherbourg, and has become involved with several American Negroes as the result of a theft at a bar. "So many smart men go to pieces nowadays," Nicole smugly remarks of Abe (99), in a judgment that looks forward not only to Dick's collapse but to its similar conclusion in a drunken scrape. The group is now rapidly descending to each member's base level of weakness of temperament. Nicole is growing increasingly tense over Dick's enchantment with Rosemary, Dick is increasingly "demoniac and frightened" (104) by his conflicting commitments to Nicole and Rosemary, and Rosemary is increasingly conscious of the deep feelings she has stirred up through her girlish crush on Dick. Fitzgerald thus establishes a symbolic resonance on this last day in Paris between the confusion and violence of Abe's imbroglio with the black community in Paris, leading to the death of an innocent man, and the emotional chaos of the triangle that has now fully emerged, leading to the violent scene in the Divers' hotel bathroom.

Equally central to the elaborately choreographed climax of the Paris visit, in which Abe's difficulties and the triangle of Rosemary, Dick, and Nicole are skillfully interwoven, is a powerful sexual symbolism. As Rosemary and Dick sit kissing on her hotel bed, with Nicole in her room across the hall—it is only three days since Rosemary astonished Dick with her "Take me" in the same room—they are no longer blind to the deceptions that have ruled their relationship. Rosemary has become aware of Dick's role of poised control, and Dick has become aware that Rosemary is playing out a film role of youthful romance. "Oh, we're such *actors*—you and I," Rosemary tells him—the "most sincere thing" she has said to him (105).

They are interrupted—with Dick guiltily smoothing the bed on which they have been sitting—by Abe and Mr. Peterson, the black man with whom Abe is involved in the case of mistaken identity stemming from the bar theft. Dick takes Abe, Peterson, and Rosemary to his suite, and Peterson offers to wait in the hall while they discuss the matter. When Abe leaves, "Dick and Rosemary embraced fleetingly. There was a dust of Paris over both of them" (108). This is their last embrace until three years later, when they meet in Rome at a very different stage in their lives, and Fitzgerald wishes to make clear, by means of an image he found especially evocative—one recalls the "foul dust" that besmirches Gatsby—the transformation that has occurred between Antibes and this moment. Gatsby's "dust" of vulgar display and suspiciously acquired wealth disguises the essential greatness of his tragic quest. The "dust of Paris," on the other hand, covers the super-ficial and contrived "glow" of Dick and Rosemary in the ideal roles they have picked for themselves and symbolizes the true state of their emotional and moral lives: all, including Nicole, have in the Paris moment had their tragic flaws raised to the surface and made fully operative in their lives.

When the problem appears at least temporarily resolved—Abe and Peterson are to go into hiding until the case of mistaken identity is cleared up—Rosemary returns to her room, only to find Peterson dead on her bed. She summons Dick, who notices Peterson's blood on her coverlet and blanket. Dick's highest priority is saving Rosemary from any link with the crime. Once again, and now climactically, Dick will play the wise and strong protector of innocence. But to do that means neglecting or discarding Nicole, as Dick in effect does when he involves Nicole in the affair by asking her to replace Rosemary's bloodstained bedclothes with clean bedclothes from one of their beds. The sexual dynamics of the scene now become painfully and violently evident. The bedclothes on which Dick and Rosemary sat kissing are now bloody—in an allusion, perhaps, to a loss of virginal innocence—and the bed is to be cleansed of its stain by the substitution of Nicole's bedclothes. To Nicole, Dick's request has to signify her replacement by Rosemary. Her response, as at Antibes, is to retreat to the bathroom in hysterics, a place and act which both she and Dick accept as a sign of her need and his duty. This is a moment when desperate and sterile sexual needs intersect: Rosemary's for a father figure, Dick's for an adoring and ego-flattering love, and Nicole's for complete possession of Dick. The bloody bedclothes passing between the three are a melodramatic but apt symbol of the sexual warfare in which the figure ostensibly in control, Dick, is instead the chief victim—equally in the failure of his reaching-out for Rosemary and in his submission once again to Nicole's emotional blackmail. Despite having kissed a beautiful young movie star in her hotel room and having recently had sex with his wife, it is he who is being emasculated in spirit. Both Rosemary and Nicole will eventually dispose of him as a worn-out shell, his creative energy permanently drained.

The Paris section of *Tender Is the Night* concludes with Rosemary— who has seen and heard Nicole in the bathroom—fleeing in dismay and fear, with Dick again fully ensnared by Nicole, and with Nicole all-powerful in her illness. What was obscure in the bathroom scene at Antibes is now clear, though the origins of the Divers' malaise in their early experience are still to be revealed. Fitzgerald has skillfully and evocatively used the sites and tourist experience of the well-to-do Right Bank to the same basic effect as Hemingway used the sites and expatriate experience of the bohemian Left Bank. Instead of Montparnasse cafés and small restaurants and working-class dance halls, now the Ritz Bar, large and expensive hotels, and fashionable shops situate what happens.[9] The different settings of *Tender Is the Night* and *The Sun Also Rises* nevertheless serve as the context for the dramatization of a similar malaise of the spirit, a malaise rendered largely by the sexual symbolism arising from the interaction of the characters and the Paris scene. Fitzgerald, however, in depicting his own version of a wasteland of the spirit, depends less than Hemingway on explicit geographical symbolism, such as journeys from the Seine to Montparnasse, and more on the symbolic implications of a sequence of actions within a specific site. The revelation of Dick's futile desire to renew himself by living out the lost codes of the past in the present—in contrast to Jake, who has accepted their loss—occurs, for example, within the gradual exposure of this need in furtive meetings with Rosemary in taxis and hotel rooms. And Rosemary's understanding of Nicole's power and underlying anger is revealed by the increasing tension in their shopping excursions.

9. *Tender Is the Night* may, however, allude to a Left Bank setting of *The Sun Also Rises* when Nicole and Abe reminisce in the Gare Saint-Lazare and he recalls the "afternoon you took me to that funny ball—you know, St. Geneviève's" (80). Possibly this is a reference to the *bal musette* on the rue de la Montagne Sainte-Geneviève, not far from the place de la Contrescarpe, that Jake and Brett attend early in *The Sun Also Rises*. There is perhaps a further homage to *The Sun Also Rises* later in *Tender Is the Night* when a stage of the Tour de France bicycle race arrives in Cannes just as Tommy Barban and Nicole are to announce their love to Dick. The event recalls the professional bicycle tour that Jake encounters at San Sebastian after he leaves the *feria* at Pamplona.

It is thus especially appropriate that the climax of the Paris moment for the Diver group occurs in hotel bedrooms. The Paris hotel room is a traditional site both of the sexual assignation (as in Nin's and Miller's works) and of farce comedy (as in the French bedroom farce). The conditions for both assignation and farce exist in the opening of the final scene: the lovers kissing in one room, the jealous wife close by in another. But instead of the comforting, expected closure of consummated passion or its comic thwarting, the moment collapses into wrenching frustration and hysteria.

The remainder of *Tender Is the Night* occupies two time frames: an initial brief section on Nicole and Dick from their meeting in 1917 to the summer of 1925 at Antibes, just as Rosemary arrives; and a lengthy section of approximately half the novel on the Divers from immediately after the Paris trip to their separation in the summer of 1929. Both sections depend heavily on the Paris section of the novel. The first makes clear the origin of the events in Paris; the second traces their consequences.

What becomes especially plain as we encounter Dick and Nicole in 1917 and follow them to their marriage two years later is the almost deterministic cast of their lives. Dick, out of his bred-in-the-bones chivalric frame of mind and the complementary need to be valued, is irresistibly drawn to the youthful, beautiful, and needful Nicole. And Nicole, having been severely scarred by her father, who was himself drawn by her innocence and vulnerability, is now compulsively seeking a more legitimate protector as well as one whom she can control through her wealth.

Fitzgerald throughout this section makes felt the underlying ominousness of the seemingly pure and generous emotions that are bringing Dick and Nicole together. Not only are Dick's fellow psychiatrists disturbed by his permitting transference to slip into personal relationship, but even more pointedly, the behavior of Baby Warren, Nicole's sister, and Devereux Warren, her father, gives broad hints of the implications of Dick's absorption into the Warren sphere. Baby Warren, in her cold-blooded willingness to use Dick for the Warrens' purposes and to discard him when his usefulness has passed, foreshadows Nicole at full strength. And Devereux Warren's susceptibility to his daughter, despite his scruples as a father, anticipates the overlay of troubled guilt that will color Dick's response to Nicole throughout their relationship. For Dick and Nicole, the complications of acting out the emotions of

Daddy's Girl have been exerting their pressure long before Rosemary's appearance.

Just as the events of the summer of 1925 which begin the novel are centered on two places, Antibes and Paris, so Dick's collapse, from 1925 to 1929, is dramatized principally by the extended sections devoted to Dick in Rome in late 1928 and in Antibes in the summer of 1929. Nicole safeguards her victory over Dick and Rosemary in several ways between the summer of 1925 and the fall of 1928. She reasserts her economic power and Dick's dependence on it when she subsidizes his purchase of a partnership in a Swiss clinic, and she reasserts her emotional dependence on him through her continuing illness, which flares at times into spells of baseless hysterical jealousy. (The wife of Dick's Swiss colleague remarks, "I think that Nicole is less sick than any one thinks. . . . She ought to be in the cinema"; 237–38.) Dick himself is forced to acknowledge, with a suggestive symbolism, that his "spear had been blunted" (201) by his years with Nicole, in which his dependence both on her wealth and on his own gratifying role of protector of the young and impressionable has increased.

It is at this point, in the fall of 1928, that Dick receives two memento mori with significant implications for his own state. Abe North, he learns, has died in a speakeasy brawl in New York, fulfilling the expectations present in his Paris visit and providing as well a portent for Dick, given his own blighted career and increased drinking. And Dick's father, the last repository for Dick of the values of the past that have been debased by the war, also dies. It is in a mood of personal futility and self-contempt, therefore, that Dick accidentally encounters Rosemary in Rome. They consummate their relationship at last, though more in the spirit of collecting on an overdue debt than with the passion of Paris. Both realize — while playing out the gestures of love — the emptiness of the deed, and afterward, in a self-destructive pattern reminiscent of Abe North, Dick gets drunk, assaults a police officer, and is badly beaten and arrested. The nadir of Dick's collapse, in a moment of epiphany with a powerful surreal undercurrent, occurs when he is being led into court. A crowd is waiting to jeer a child rapist who is also to appear that morning. The battered and desheveled Dick is momentarily mistaken for the rapist, and he quickly goes along with the misidentification in tragicomic self-recognition. "I want to make a speech," Dick says. "I want to explain to these people how I raped a five-year-old girl. Maybe I did—" (236).

The last phase of Dick's European years, from late 1928 to the summer of 1929, dramatizes concretely the despair that marked his Rome experience. His drinking pushes on to where it becomes a form of self-punishment, and he is forced to give up his clinic and return to Antibes. There, Nicole's underlying Warren strength and hardness begin to control the narrative, and accordingly there is a shift to her point of view. Dick's weakness makes him less and less useful, while her increasing self-confidence—derived in part from her ability to dominate him—make him expendable. More as a test of her own independence and power than out of any full-scale passion, she begins the affair with Tommy Barban that precipitates the dismissal of Dick from her life.

The final scenes of the novel unfold where the story began, at Antibes, with Dick feebly and pathetically seeking to repeat the gestures that so charmed Rosemary four years earlier. He fails miserably in his efforts to show off his physical prowess, and the imperative he is under to play the gentleman protector to those in difficulty obtains its outlet not with an ingenuous and appreciative Rosemary but with a lesbian Englishwoman and a hardened Mary North, who despise him while using him. So Dick visits the beach on the morning of his last day at Antibes and views his now lost kingdom and its subjects. With the exception of Abe North, all the principal figures of the earlier stay at Antibes are present. He is slightly drunk, and as he prepares to leave, he provides a last negative epiphany. He "raised his right hand and with a papal cross he blessed the beach" (312). The Prospero who seemed to exist in a timeless magic world has been revealed by the crucible of Paris to be a common mortal vulnerable to history and to himself. He has nevertheless returned to his former realm for one last ironic gesture of poised control.

THE MOMENT SYNTHESIZED

Henry Miller
Tropic of Cancer

Tropic of Cancer not only is a relatively late example of American expatriate writing between the wars but also constitutes a synthesis of the various strands I have noted in the expatriate representation of the Paris moment. Themes whose prominence in other works owe much to their generic siting—the autobiographical stress on a birth of creative potency within the Paris scene, the fictional on various kinds of failure of this capacity—are here equally prominent within a single work in which, indeed, autobiography and fiction blend and become indistinguishable in the author's single-minded pursuit of the essential expatriate subject matter of Paris as a crucible for the refining of the creative spirit into gold or dross. *Tropic of Cancer* is also a synthesis in the sense that Miller heightens into an almost unremitting presence the principal metaphoric analogues provided by the Paris scene for the expression of these themes. What are largely tropes in the writing of the other expatriates—the implications for the creative imagination of feasting and mobility within the Paris moment—become for Miller, by means of the picaresque adventures of his artist-hero, the very substance of the work.[1]

1. Miller has received a good deal of attention, much of it biographical or polemical, in recent decades. Among biographies, see Jay Martin, *Always Merry and Bright: The Life of Henry Miller* (Santa Barbara, Calif., 1978), and Robert Ferguson, *Henry Miller: A Life* (New York, 1991). These works identify the prototypes of the various figures in *Tropic of Cancer*. The most useful criticism of *Tropic of Cancer* includes William A. Gordon's *The Mind and Art of Henry Miller* (Baton Rouge, 1967), Leon Lewis' *Henry Miller: The Major Writings* (New York, 1986), Jean Méral's *Paris in*

Miller's belief that to break loose from the imprisoning sterility of American life required conscious acts of rebellion influenced him to adopt in *Tropic of Cancer* a modernist imitative form of a seeming chaos, in which fiction and autobiography are indistinguishable, plot and chronological order are almost undetectable, and social realism, high lyricism, and surreal reverie mix freely. Thus, readers encountering *Tropic of Cancer* for the first time are often disturbed not only by its explicit sexual and scatological language but also by its shapelessness. We are introduced to an impoverished and footloose American living in Paris whose thoughts, feelings, recollections, and experience are narrated to us in discontinuous fragments. In accord with, it would seem, an impulse to show first and tell later, the first part of the work is especially chaotic: time, place, and subject matter often shift radically after a few paragraphs.[2] The later sections, on the other hand, present lengthier incidents and offer much comment on the form and technique of the book. "My idea," Miller tells us in one of his later explanatory passages, "has been to get off the gold standard of literature. My idea briefly has been to present a resurrection of the emotions."[3] The "gold standard" of art would appear to involve the traditionally valued ideals of order, symmetry, restraint, and proportion. For Miller, these are false ideals, for they distance art from the turbulence and disorder of life, especially of the inner life. He is also disturbed by the endorsement of conventional beliefs that a writer's adoption of conventional form may imply. Soon after his comment on a gold standard of art, he writes, "When I reflect that the task which the artist implicitly sets himself is to overthrow existing values, to make of the chaos about him an order which is his own, to sow strife and ferment so that by the emotional release those who are dead may be restored to life, then it is that I run with joy to the great and imperfect ones, their confusion nourishes me, their stuttering is like divine music to my ears" (253).

As is true, however, of many writers who affirm that their work is the spontaneous expression of instinctive emotions—Whitman is an

---

American Literature (Chapel Hill, N.C., 1989), and *Critical Essays on Henry Miller*, ed. Ronald Gottesman (New York, 1992). Some valuable commentary on Miller and his work is also sprinkled throughout Anaïs Nin's diaries and letters of the early 1930s.

2. Miller responds to the reader's presumed dismay at encountering this disorder by assuming a pose of writing spontaneously and without revision. "I have made a silent compact with myself not to change a line of what I write," he notes a few pages into *Tropic of Cancer*. We know, of course, that the work was extensively revised.

3. *Tropic of Cancer* (1934; rpr. New York, 1961), 243. Further citations of this edition will appear in the text.

instructive example—Miller disguises in his aesthetic of chaos a carefully shaped and modulated principle of form. Since Miller's disparate Paris experiences feature bizarre incidents with few reappearing figures, the picaresque, which achieves its shape through the extraordinary adventures of a genial rogue hero, would appear to be the best candidate for a principle of form in *Tropic of Cancer*. But to stress the picaresque as controlling shape in the work is to lessen a recognition that Miller's adventures do not progress toward a goal—the typical picaresque closure of newfound wealth or marriage or the solution of a mystery—but rather conclude as they began, with Miller alive, well, and happy in Paris. When we encounter Miller at the opening of *Tropic of Cancer,* he announces that he is poor, a free spirit, and an artist, that he is exhilarated by this state, and that he is "pregnant" with the book we are now reading (26). There is no advance in this condition in the course of the work, and therefore the usual forward thrust of narrative—of explainable change occurring through the course of time, that is, of plot—is absent from *Tropic of Cancer.* What replaces it, and what in effect replaces the awareness of time as the matrix of the work, is a sense of place—of Paris as a world of variety, richness, and freedom of experience beyond anything Miller has previously encountered. Put in other terms, Miller in *Tropic of Cancer* fills in a space rather than tells a story. The space is Paris, and he is its perceiving consciousness. Since his response to the city is emotional, and since the city in its varied and fragmented character occasions many different emotions—from wonder to despair—chaos is almost inevitably the operative aesthetic of his spatial form.

Miller's employment of a spatial form in *Tropic of Cancer* therefore amounts to a conscious rejection of the customary structuring device of chronology. Not only are events narrated with no effort to place them in a coherent time frame, but timelessness in the sense of Miller's many chronologically unpegged passages of anecdotal recollection and surreal reverie reinforces the sense that *Tropic of Cancer* is an imaginative construct in which time is of no import.[4] *Tropic of Cancer* thus exhibits

4. Although Miller always allowed himself great freedom in re-creating the events of his life in his writing, the exceptionally loose and misleading chronology he gives in *Tropic of Cancer* for his initial years in Paris can also be attributed to his attempt to establish the effect of a timeless unity for the moment. Miller mentions no dates in *Tropic of Cancer,* but the work ostensibly begins in the early fall of 1931, when Miller has been in Paris for a year and a half—he arrived in early 1930—and is beginning to write the book. It presumably ends in the spring of 1932, after his return from Dijon. Within this half year, Miller packs both a year and a half of seasonal changes and a number of circumstances, such as his living with Fillmore, that occurred before the opening

in extreme form a major characteristic of expatriate writing which I have already noted in *A Moveable Feast* and *The Autobiography of Alice B. Toklas:* the trading of the effect of causality which derives from a coherent movement through time for the powerful effect of an unchanging response to a place which a fragmentation of the response into its parts can produce. Miller's theme that Paris is a metaphor of the creative life reaches us in a rush of mixed fragments—mixed in tone and fragmented in subject matter—that nevertheless constitute a "truth" about both his feelings and the nature of the city. For Miller in *Tropic of Cancer,* in brief, Paris as mythic moment is both the theme and form of the work.

There is also a specific likeness between the spatial forms of *A Moveable Feast* and *Tropic of Cancer* in that both works give meaning to their space—and to what it is to be a writer in Paris during the 1920s and 1930s—through a series of polarized portraits of other Paris artists and friends. But whereas Hemingway restricts himself to people he knew during his Paris years and then parcels them out as saints and sinners, Miller also draws upon artists of the past and refers to them in distinguishing between those who do and those who do not profitably avail themselves of the Paris moment. The figures of Miller's own Paris—the writers and would-be writers of his own day who are an important side of his Paris world—fail in various ways to tap the rich vein of creative energy that runs through the Paris scene, and they are the object of his contempt.[5] But he believes that some earlier artists acted courageously in the role of outsider and rebel he envisions for himself, and it is these who serve as his icons of inspiration. A few, such as August Strindberg, were also expatriates in Paris, but most—like Henri Matisse and Walt Whitman—serve as models in that they heroically forged a new and revolutionary art despite a resisting bourgeoisie. Miller's dichotomy between courageous rebellion and thin posturing, in which examples of the first exist principally in his memory and in his consciousness of his own stance and examples of the second overrun the artistic world with which he has direct personal acquaint-

---

of the work in the early fall of 1931. In short, Miller is not interested, and does not wish the reader to be interested, in an accurate or even a discernible chronology.

5. Miller's satiric rendering of all his fellow expatriates—even his friend Carl (Alfred Perlès) is negatively depicted—may explain why Nin, whom he met in late 1930, does not appear. Of course, Miller had personal reasons for leaving Nin out, since his affair with her was continuing and she still lived with her husband. But he also no doubt realized that to include a figure with a responsiveness to Paris like his own would compromise the strategy of posing the artist-hero against a series of foils.

ance, lends a distinctive cast to the spatialization of the Paris expatriate experience in *Tropic of Cancer*. As artist-hero carrying the banners of freedom, honesty, and vitality, Miller everywhere encounters the opposites of these qualities in actual experience, but he maintains inviolate within himself, with the aid of avatars from the past, a sacred integrity of the spirit. In one of the frequently misunderstood paradoxes of *Tropic of Cancer*, Miller, in a Paris filled with those whose debasing of the expatriate ideal of freedom besmirches a faith almost religious in its essential character, nevertheless maintains through his own active belief in this ideal a form of chivalric, and indeed sacred, quest for its fulfillment.

Miller's representation of the Paris moment can be clarified by reference to three sections of *Tropic of Cancer* that in relation to one another offer a compressed illustration of the quest motif in the work as a whole. These are a passage on Matisse, in which the ideal configuration of the artist in Paris is suggested; a more extended section recounting Miller's experiences with a follower of Gandhi, in which the distinctive character of Miller's own creative life in Paris becomes clear; and a lengthy account of Van Norden, in which Miller's device of using his Paris acquaintances as foils for his own values as an artist is evident. The three passages, since they occur not in immediate succession but at three separate points in the narrative, also exhibit that aspect of the modernist spatial form of *Tropic of Cancer* according to which a single coherent "argument"—about the origin, nature, and desecration of a personal ethos—is represented in fragmented form within the total space of Miller's Paris moment.

At the opening of the section about Matisse, Miller comments on the prevalence of the misshapen and maimed on the streets of large cities, "men and women whose last drop of juice has been squeezed out by the machine—the martyrs of modern progress" (162). Although Miller does not cite New York here, he throughout *Tropic of Cancer* associates the baneful consequences of the mechanization of life in the name of progress with New York and with American civilization in general. New York "is cold, glittering, malign. The buildings dominate. There is a sort of atomic frenzy to the activity going on; the more furious the pace, the more diminished the spirit" (68). In contrast, in a Paris gallery filled with Matisses, Miller feels himself "drawn back again to the proper precincts of the human world" from the death-in-life of the mechanized city. The "color of life" (162) splashes forth from Matisse' paintings and thereby signifies their refusal to participate in the "consummation of death" (163).

Matisse shows how an artist can not only champion the color of life against the pallor of death but also exhibit the "courage to sacrifice an harmonious line in order to detect the rhythm and murmur of the blood" (164). And blood in Matisse, Miller infers from his violent colors and luxuriant odalisques, is not a matter of "feline beauty," that is, of a genteel aesthetic of the kind "which has us by the balls in America." The beauty of Matisse' art lies rather in his fidelity to the flow of life— not only to blood, Miller explains, but also to seminal fluid and excrement, to any bodily movement that symbolizes the vitality of the spirit in contrast to the image of a soul encased in concrete. Miller pursues the image: "To fathom the new reality it is first necessary to dismantle the drains, to lay open the gangrened ducts which compose the genito-urinary system that supplies the excreta of art" (165).

In Matisse' paintings lie both a vital art of the past and the hope for a similar art in the future. And Matisse' Paris still exists as a fecund context for the expression of a living art; his vision of what he saw has had its effect on what can still be seen: "In the evenings now and then, skirting the cemetery walls, I stumble upon the phantom odalisques of Matisse fastened to the trees, their tangled manes drenched with sap" (166). He adds, "Even as the world falls apart the Paris that belonged to Matisse shudders with bright, gasping orgasms, the air itself is steady with a stagnant sperm, the trees tangled like hair" (166).

Miller establishes through Matisse a fully developed paradigm for the artist-hero. To grasp life as an artist is to speak for the principle of flow in life, of freedom and rebelliousness in theme and form, including above all the sexual as the supreme image of a rebellious fluidity. And Paris, through its richness and variety of life, can supply instances both of those who have permitted themselves to be captured by and made one with the static and mechanical in modern life (a Van Norden, for example) and those who have made themselves part of the flow (Miller, above all), thus confirming that "the revolution is intact" (166).

Miller's fullest account of his own participation in a Matisse-like quest for an art of "life" within the Paris moment, with Paris serving both as a stimulus to the creative imagination and as a reservoir of imagery available to document the health of that faculty, occurs in a long section early in *Tropic of Cancer* which deals with his relationship to the Hindu community of Paris (78–99). The first figure introduced, Nanantatee, sits for one of Miller's characteristically satiric portraits. Like almost all

A Paris house of prostitution ("Chez Suzy") in the early thirties
Photograph by Brassaï. Copyright © Estate Brassaï.

of those whom the artist-hero meets in his adventures, from the death-obsessed Boris of the opening to the self-destructively sentimental Fillmore at the close, he serves as a foil to the cast of mind and spirit of the artist-hero and is thus a subject for caricature. Nanantatee is miserly, gross, and lazy, but he delights in playing the role of a spiritually pure and generous host, all the while exploiting and demeaning the dependent Miller. The portrait flows into what initially appears to be an extended comic anecdote about another sanctimonious Hindu, an unnamed follower of Gandhi who is in Europe to raise money for his master. The young disciple is vain and pompous, and he has also been wearied by his labors and requires the solace of a visit to a whorehouse, which it falls to Miller to provide. In a farcical incident, the Indian mistakes a bidet for a toilet and produces two large turds, to the dismay of the prostitute and the madam. Several nights later, Miller again accompanies the disciple as he goes in pursuit of the "fucking business" (94). Once they are settled in a low dive of a brothel, Miller begins a reverie on the earlier visit. Man, he realizes, has devoted his energy throughout his existence in pursuit of miracles to confirm impossible beliefs:

And out of the endless torment and misery no miracle comes forth, no microscopic vestige even of relief. Only ideas, pale, attenuated ideas which have to be fattened [for] slaughter; ideas which come forth like bile, like the guts of a pig when the carcass is ripped open.

And so I think what a miracle it would be if this miracle which man attends eternally should turn out to be nothing more than these two enormous turds which the faithful disciple dropped in the *bidet*. What if at the last moment, when the banquet table is set and the cymbals clash, there should appear suddenly, and wholly without warning, a silver platter on which even the blind could see that there is nothing more, and nothing less, than two enormous lumps of shit. . . .

Somehow the realization that nothing was to be hoped for had a salutary effect upon me. For weeks and months, for years, in fact, all my life I had been looking forward to something happening, some extrinsic event that would alter my life, and now suddenly, inspired by the absolute hopelessness of everything, I felt relieved, felt as though a great burden had been lifted from my shoulders. . . . Walking toward Montparnasse I decided to let myself drift with the tide, to make not the least resistance to fate, no matter in what form it presented itself. Nothing that had happened to me thus far had been sufficient to destroy me; nothing had been destroyed except my illusions. I myself was intact. . . . I made up my mind that I would hold on to nothing, that I would expect nothing, that henceforth I would live as an animal, a beast of prey, a rover, a plunderer. . . . One must burrow into life again to put on flesh. The word must become flesh; the soul thirsts. On whatever crumb my eye fastens, I will pounce and devour. If to live is the paramount thing, then I will live, even if I must become a cannibal. Heretofore I have been trying to save my precious hide, trying to preserve the few pieces of meat that hid my bones. I am done with that. I have reached the limits of endurance. My back is to the wall; I can retreat no further. As far as history goes I am dead. If there is something beyond I shall have to bounce back. I have found God, but he is insufficient. I am only spiritually dead. Physically I am alive. Morally I am free. The world which I have departed is a menagerie. The dawn is breaking on a new world, a jungle world in which the lean spirits roam with sharp claws. If I am a hyena I am a lean and hungry one: I go forth to fatten myself. (97–99)

Miller has in this passage crystallized, within a whorehouse setting and an imagery of cannibalism that both relies on and parodies the traditional motifs and language of religious mysticism, the essence of his creative rebirth in Paris. Throughout history, he now understands, the search for transcendent meaning in life has produced only *merde*. Recognition of this forces him into an acceptance of life and man as they are, free of cant and convention. And in this acceptance of life, this burrowing into it, the thirst for the spiritual meaning of life will paradoxically be met. Miller dramatizes a moment of mystical insight that began with two turds in a Paris brothel and ended with a new strength of creative freedom and power arising out of his acceptance of the elemental union of body and soul. The soul itself, within that acceptance, is not defiled in its role as hyena. Rather, in a hyena's ravenous hunger and relentless pursuit, Miller in his own way echoes the feeding and mobility tropes that pervade a positive view of the potential of the Paris moment.

The hyena of the spirit—to take Miller's image to its logical conclusion within the context of *Tropic of Cancer* as a whole—flourishes when it pursues its prey relentlessly and devours it when it has run it down. I have already noted Miller's endorsement of the ethos of mobility and fluidity he finds in Matisse, and I will return to that trope later. But I would like now to discuss what is one of the most distinctive characteristics of *Tropic of Cancer* as expatriate expression, Miller's bold and open transformation of the expatriate trope of feeding into one of above all sexual hunger.[6]

6. Miller occasionally uses a comic version of the association between food and sex, as when he writes, "I have never seen a place like Paris for varieties of sexual provender" (162).

The tendency among all the writers I have discussed to establish a metaphoric association between sexual and creative potency takes on a literalness in *Tropic of Cancer* that often obscures a recognition of Miller's symbolic intent. In an extraordinary variety of narrated incidents, expressionistic reveries, and authorial asides, sex as male desire drives the theme of acceptance of life as it is which constitutes the heart of the artist-hero's quest for understanding and fulfillment. Miller's own unrelenting sexuality—his permanent horniness and its necessary outlet, for a man of his circumstances, either in daydreams or whores—is one aspect of his personal hunger. But far more meaningful in the unfolding of Miller's basic sexual theme is his distinction between his own "honest" sexuality and a sexuality that perverts or denies its own central place in all that is creative within the human spirit. He therefore opens *Tropic of Cancer* with a combination of grandiose pronouncements about his artistic aims and a number of gross sexual daydreams and anecdotes. The artist who will later demand that we get off the gold standard of literature immediately tests our willingness to do so by plunging us into his sexual metaphor.

Sex as physical energy, social truth, and spiritual force pervades *Tropic of Cancer* and affords a basis for the frequent comparison—encouraged by Miller himself—between the work and some of Whitman's greatest poems. Miller's turning of the whorehouse into a scene of self-discovery can be considered a striking and provocative extension into modern Paris of Whitman's man in the open air freeing himself from worn-out creeds and embracing as a new faith both his own spirit and all that exists in nature. Although Miller is indeed often radical in his subject matter and language, he follows many of his fellow American expatriate writers in not so much expressing a new faith as restating traditional beliefs within the striking contexts that the Paris scene grants. But Miller also differs markedly from Whitman in devoting less attention to the celebration of a "positive" sexuality—think of the Whitman of "I Sing the Body Electric"—than to the satiric caricature of its opposite. "Negative" sexual portraits in a multiplicity of forms constitute one of the major motifs in *Tropic of Cancer*. In one manifestation of the motif, Miller's desire creates an implicit comparison between a productive and an impotent sexuality, as when his daydreams about the voluptuous Tania occur in the context of her husband Sylvester, a successful but effete writer of popular plays. In another, Miller stands somewhat aside, as in the comparison between the whores Germaine and Claude. And in the most frequent manifestation, he is present almost entirely as an observer, as in his lengthy account of the perversion of human sexuality that is Van Norden.

The comparison of Germaine and Claude, part of Miller's recollection early in the work of these two whores, whom he encountered soon after arriving in Paris, is a good example of his manipulation of sexual material in the service of themes of artistic creativity. Of the two prostitutes, Germaine has no false modesty or shame; she glories in her professional equipment, puts her "heart and soul into her work" (47), and "connects" with life (45). "However vile and circumscribed was that world which she had created for herself," Miller writes, "nevertheless she functioned in it superbly. And that in itself is a tonic thing" (46). On the other hand, "with Claude there was always a certain delicacy, even when she got under the sheets with you. And her delicacy offended. Who wants a *delicate* whore! . . . Germaine had the right idea. . . . She was a whore all the way through—and that was her virtue!" (47).

Germaine and Claude exemplify two poles of value in *Tropic of Cancer.* Germaine is Miller in his vibrant acceptance and celebration of life and of himself as he has found them; Claude is almost any of the other figures in the work, those locked into false and life-denying codes and values. Boris' preoccupation with death and Moldorf's abstract philosophizing and Carl's covetousness are all represented by Claude. And each of these poles—especially the "positive" one of a Whitman-esque faith in the physical life as symbolic of spiritual richness—is intrinsically linked to an aesthetic ideal that it is the function of the artist-hero to celebrate when he finds it and condemn when he discovers it violated.

The most striking condemnation of its violation by means of a foil figure occurs in Miller's portrait of Van Norden.[7] This account, the longest in *Tropic of Cancer* devoted to a figure other than Miller, has frequently been misread by those eager to attack Miller as sexually obsessed and a degrader of women. To read the section along these lines, however, is to disregard both Miller's use of the foil technique throughout *Tropic of Cancer* and its specific application in this instance. At one point in the portrait, Van Norden praises Miller as a "good listener" (132), and indeed he is, his principal role in the section being to record Van Norden's monologues. Those reveal, through direct quote

7. Van Norden is based on the American newspaperman Wambly Bald, who wrote a gossip column for the Paris *Tribune* during this period.

and free indirect discourse, that it is Van Norden himself in his pose as world-weary nihilist who feels himself imprisoned by sex and as a result demeans the women he considers his jailers. "No matter what he does or where he goes," Miller reports, using an indirect-discourse literalism to render Van Norden's obscene habit of mind and speech, "things are out of joint. Either it's the fucking country or the fucking job, or else it's some fucking cunt who's put him on the blink" (101).

Van Norden resembles Fitzgerald in Hemingway's depiction of him in *A Moveable Feast* and Cohn in *The Sun Also Rises*. He is an expatriate anti-Christ in the sense that almost every aspect of his character and life runs counter to the potential of Paris to nourish and fulfill the artist. He is a writer, but he makes his living reporting gossip for a Paris newspaper. He frequents Montparnasse cafés, and he has never been in the Louvre. He has a bad stomach and has to be careful about his diet. He is not poor, but he lives in sordid conditions out of self-contempt and a contempt for others. And most of all, he is proccupied by sex but cannot feel love or passion.

The portrait reaches its culmination when Van Norden and Miller bring a whore to Van Norden's room. "We haven't any passion either of us. And as for her, one might as well expect her to produce a diamond necklace as to show a spark of passion. But there's the fifteen francs and something has to be done about it. It's like a state of war" (142). Miller withdraws from the combat, but Van Norden perseveres. "As I watch Van Norden tackle her, it seems to me that I'm looking at a machine whose cogs have slipped. Left to themselves, they could go on this way forever, grinding and slipping without anything happening. Until a hand shuts the motor off" (144). In his role as observer and moralist within his foil construct, Miller then sententiously comments, "As long as that spark of passion is missing there is no human significance in the performance. The machine is better to watch" (144). For both Miller and Van Norden, the sexual freedom of Paris provides the opportunity for many kinds of sexual association, from prostitution to casual affairs to extended relationships. But unlike Miller, for whom desire signifies an emotional need and hence the tapping of the energized center of his nature, Van Norden experiences sex as empty and mechanical—a kind of meaningless war—and his participation in it is merely one more facet of the enervation of the spirit of the whole man.

If Van Norden embodies one kind of misshapen expatriate sexuality, Fillmore, in the long closing section of the book, represents another. Fillmore is so taken with the glamour of his role as expatriate—he is banker by day and bohemian by night—that he repeatedly permits the sexual sharks patrolling the Montparnasse waters to victimize him. We encounter this susceptibility initially in a shaggy-dog story in which a self-styled Russian countess lives off him while she keeps coming up with reasons not to make love—she has gonorrhea, she says, she is a lesbian, she is too small—until he wearies and loses interest. His greatest misadventure, however, occurs with Ginette, a hard-boiled prostitute who plays the innocent country girl in an effort to trick him into marrying her.

Miller, in the large portion of *Tropic of Cancer* devoted to Van Norden and Fillmore, is far more the observer than the participant. As observer, he is extending into the very core of the work his image of himself as a hyena in the Paris jungle. He is not an active force in the lives of Van Norden and Fillmore and other similar figures; he has not contributed to their wounding, that is, to their failure as expatriates. But he is feeding on them in the sense of observing their failings and translating these into a confirmation of his own ethos as a sharp-eyed yet exultant celebrator of expatriate life as he has found it. He has nourished his own art on the carcasses of his fellows.

Yet, despite the importance of the feeding image in *Tropic of Cancer,* especially in its sexual extension, Miller's principal trope for Paris as a source of artistic freedom, growth, and strength is, as in Nin's *Diary,* that of flow.[8] For Miller, however, the conflict between the inertia of conformist belief and thought and the primal energy of freedom assumes a different shape from Nin's model of a Louveciennes of torpor and a Paris of spontaneity and intuitiveness. To move and thus to live as an artist is, for Miller, above all to wander the quartiers of Paris. He recalls in *Tropic of Cancer* his arrival in Paris, alone and poor and therefore "wandering and wandering" (16). "My world of human beings," he later comments, "had perished. I was utterly alone in the world and for friends I had the streets, and the streets spoke to me in that sad, bitter language compounded of human misery, yearning, regret, failure, wasted effort" (184).

---

8. It is of some interest that Nin herself, in her preface to the first edition of *Tropic of Cancer,* in 1934, points out the centrality of these two images. "The book," she writes, "is sustained on its own axis by the pure flux and rotation of events. Just as there is no central point, so there is no question of heroism or of struggle, since there is no question of will, but only an obedience to flow" (xxxii). She continues, "The humiliations and defeats, given with a primitive honesty, end not in frustration, despair, or futility, but in hunger, an esctatic, devouring hunger—*for more life.*"

In this remark, Miller is expressing a version of the romantic aesthetic of a Wordsworth or an Emerson, in which the writer's feeling relationship with the outer world—nature for them, the streets for Miller—provides access in symbolic form to essential truths about both oneself and experience. Indeed, Miller intimates the connection between his and Emerson's idea of correspondence—of the symbolic relationship between the world around us and our own inner nature—by choosing a passage from Emerson as the epigraph for *Tropic of Cancer.* "These novels," Miller quotes Emerson, "will give way, by and by, to diaries or autobiographies—captivating books, if only a man knew how to choose among what he calls his experiences that which is really his experience, and how to record truth truly." For Miller, the fictional has indeed given way largely to the autobiographical as the major impulse in his art, and he has indeed chosen that which was the central reality of his interaction with Paris—his wanderings through the city, to the extreme that *Tropic of Cancer* is almost a compendium of Paris street names—as a means of recording the basic truths of his experience. Consequently, Miller's wandering does not yield a single category of meaning. His Paris is cold and dark and it is sunny and vibrant, and he encounters on its streets that which dismays him and that which inspires. The truth of Paris for Miller, as for most of the other expatriate writers, is not in its incarnation of some specific insight into experience but in its ability to provide an intensity of response to various kinds of experience. No wonder, then, that when Miller is asked to show a visitor "his" Paris he cannot do so. His Paris, Miller realizes, is one "whose *arrondissements* are undefined, a Paris that has never existed except by virtue of my loneliness. . . . Such a huge Paris! It would take a lifetime to explore it again. This Paris, to which I alone had the key, hardly lends itself to a tour, even with the best of intentions; it is a Paris that has to be lived, that has to be experienced each day in a thousand different forms of torture, a Paris that grows inside of you like a cancer, and grows and grows until you are eaten away by it" (179).

The indeterminate yet vital centrality of Paris as the font of all-consuming meaning for the artist-hero is confirmed by the two major occasions when Miller temporarily leaves the city. On the first of these, he, Fillmore, and Fillmore's sailor friend Collins make a trip to Le Havre, where they engage in an extended debauch that concludes in a violent brawl in a bar. Le Havre is here, paradoxically, similar to the expatriate Paris of riotous good times which Miller has rejected in favor of the streets as a source of the fullness and richness of life. The second

occasion outside Paris is both more extended and sharper in its implication. The lengthy account of Miller's employment as an English-
language teacher in a Dijon lycée (267–87) is a brilliant elaboration of
his conviction that French provincial life is moribund. It is the depth
of winter, and Miller is unrelievedly cold and hungry in the fortresslike
lycée, where both students and teachers are prisoners and where eventually the pipes freeze and everyone is constipated. To return to Paris
in the spring, where he finds Carl comfortably in bed with a whore in
a cramped and dirty room, and where the discussion immediately turns
to Goethe, is to escape from cloacal stasis into flow.

Given Miller's preoccupation with the image of flow, it was perhaps
inevitable that his major symbol for the richness and freedom of Paris
is the Seine. The Seine is, of course, a street of Paris for a wanderer
because of its location in the heart of the city and its many bridges.
Miller therefore not only refers to the river constantly but also exploits,
like Hemingway, its symbolic potential. Early in *Tropic of Cancer,* as he
recalls his first weeks in Paris, he remembers a "weird sort of contentment in those days. No appointments, no invitations for dinner, no
program, no dough. The golden period, when I had not a single friend"
(16). In connection with his state of negatively described nirvana—of
exhilaration born of escaping the pressures and commitments of New
York—it is the Seine that is the primary image in his rush of recollection of the color, smell, and feel of a Paris of awakening and discovery:

> Wandering along the Seine at night . . . and going mad with the beauty
> of it, the trees leaning to, the broken images in the water, the rush of
> the current under the bloody lights of the bridges, the women sleeping
> in doorways, sleeping on newspapers, sleeping in the rain; everywhere
> the musty porches of the cathedrals and beggars and lice and old hags
> full of St. Vitus' dance; pushcarts stacked up like wine barrels in the side
> streets, the smell of berries in the market place and the old church
> surrounded with vegetables and blue arc lights, the gutters slippery with
> garbage and women in satin pumps staggering through the filth and
> vermin at the end of an all-night souse. (16)

The Seine of maddening beauty is inseparable from Parisian decay
and death, because the Paris moment caught by the river's flow contains
every variation of human experience and emotion. Sometimes, indeed,
it is rot that predominates. Standing at the window in a moment of
depression, Miller feels the "city palpitating, as if it were a heart just
removed from a warm body. The windows of my hotel are festering

and there is a thick, acrid stench as of chemicals burning. Looking into the Seine I see mud and desolation, street lamps drowning, men and women choking to death" (63–64). In any mood, though, the Seine is also a triumphant symbol of the capability of Paris to nourish the spirit of the artist-hero. Miller's usual response to the river is therefore reverence and awe, as for a sacred icon. "The river is still swollen, muddy, streaked with lights," he writes. "I don't know what it is rushes up in me at the sight of this dark, swift-moving current, but a great exultation lifts me up, affirms the deep wish that is in me never to leave this land" (67).

As the great artery of Paris, the Seine provides Miller with a powerfully evocative symbol of his belief in change and multiplicity as the dynamic core of life. Early in *Tropic of Cancer* he validates the aesthetic application of this belief in Matisse' art; toward the close he finds an even more pointed validation in James Joyce's work.

> "I love everything that flows," said the great blind Milton of our time. I was thinking of him this morning when I awoke with a great bloody shout of joy: I was thinking of his rivers and trees and all that world of night which he is exploring. Yes, I said to myself, I too love everything that flows: rivers, sewers, lava, semen, blood, bile, words, sentences. I love the amniotic fluid when it spills out of the bag. I love the kidney with its painful gallstones, its gravel and what-not; I love the urine that pours out scalding and the clap that runs endlessly; I love the words of hysterics and the sentences that flow on like dysentry and mirror all the sick images of the soul. (257)

Like Nin, who in an affirmation of flux as a principle of life closes her *Diary* of 1931–1934 with a flurry of open-ended change and movement, Miller ends *Tropic of Cancer* by returning to his own major image of flux, the Seine. He has gotten Fillmore out of his scrape with the prostitute Ginette, and using some of the money gained from that effort he treats himself to a cab ride through Paris—a kind of momentarily luxurious reprise of the "wandering and wandering" of his early days in Paris. He stops at a café and, seeing the Seine, feels a vast peace and contentment. In an epiphany, he senses himself both part of this "great artery" (318) of life and sufficiently separate from it to interpret what he has become part of:

> So quietly flows the Seine that one hardly notices its presence. It is always there, quiet and unobstrusive, like a great artery running through

the human body. In the wonderful peace that fell over me it seemed as if I had climbed to the top of a high mountain; for a little while I would be able to look around me, to take in the meaning of the landscape. . . .

The sun is setting. I feel this river flowing through me—its past, its ancient soil, the changing climate. The hills gently girdle it about: its course is fixed. (318)

The river of life that is symbolic of Paris is now inseparable from the artist-hero as affinity has become unity. But though he is indeed part of the flow of life, he has also reached a momentary resting point that has given him his sense of peace. There he can at last give birth to the perception of Paris he has reached—can write the book we are reading that expresses an affirmation both of life as flow and of the work of art as a product and model of that reality.

EPILOGUE

The works I have discussed depict Paris as a mythic rather than a historical or geographical entity. Of course, they also include much of the Paris scene between the wars that can be found in accurate scholarly accounts of the period: specific places and people and events that did exist and did occur. But the works' primary commitment is to their writers' felt response to the city as a phase in the history of their inner lives and the inner lives of their characters. The Paris of American expatriate writing is therefore not that of the monumental Paris of the occasional visitor—of Notre-Dame, the Louvre, and the Madeleine, for example—but of the quartiers and the ways of life that bear an emotional resonance for the foreigner who has settled in: Montparnasse and its café life, the shabby working-class areas of the place de la Contrescarpe and the Pantheon, the small restaurants and cafés along the Seine, and the Right Bank world of the well-to-do. This Paris ranges from Hemingway's "good café" on the place Saint-Michel and the Closerie des Lilas on the boulevard Montparnasse to Stein's atelier off the Luxembourg Gardens, the cafés where Nin and Miller talked until dawn, the Voisin's restaurant and Ritz Bar that Fitzgerald and Dos Passos knew, and Miller's countless mean streets in almost every section of the city.

This Paris of the intimately known and felt is what I have called the "Paris moment." By this term, I have meant most of all the writer's desire to invest Paris with the capacity to move him to creativity.

Stimulated by the freedom of thought and action possible within the Paris scene and nourished as well in body and spirit by the richness of Paris life, the artist finds in the Paris moment an Edenic power. Here, in this new and exhilarating world, the spirit and its attendant capacity to speak through art are reborn. Not all, however, have the strength and honesty to avail themselves of this potential. In some, the crucible of the Paris moment forces into open expression qualities of mind and spirit that have tragic consequences—especially qualities associated, as in Jake Barnes, Richard Savage, and Dick Diver, with the loss or failure of a traditional base of values and belief.

The protagonists of expatriate autobiography and fiction, though all artists or artists manqué, have suggestive implications for American culture as a whole during the period between the wars. From Hemingway not long after the war to Stein, Miller, and Nin in the 1930s, expatriate writers sought to dramatize through the Paris experiences of Americans of sensibility those qualities of life necessary to fulfill the spirit which, they either stated or implied, were not available in America. Expatriate writing is therefore often implicitly critical of specific features of American life even while obliquely celebrating other aspects of it. Hemingway, for example, could not in America of the 1920s have sat in a café having a drink and writing a story, but his escape from this limitation did not prevent him from projecting, in his account of the scene, an image of masculine sexuality deeply American in nature. Even figures who fail to draw upon the resources of the Paris moment do so largely as a result of personal weaknesses that can be considered distinctively American: the susceptibility of Fitzgerald, as portrayed by Hemingway, to the trappings of wealth, Dick Diver's self-destructive innocence, and Richard Savage's facile but self-serving "public relations" charm.

Although the depiction of the use or misuse of the capacity to benefit from the Paris moment falls into generic categories, there runs through almost all the major expatriate writing, whether fiction or autobiography, the twofold tendency to render the distinctive qualities of the moment in shared basic tropes and in spatial form. The ability of Paris to provide both freedom and nourishment for the spirit lends itself to the powerful and evocative tropes of mobility and feeding, especially in relationship to the sexual as a metaphor for creative potency. And because Paris to the expatriate writer is above all a state of mind—that is, a response to a place and its way of life by a consciousness—the form of expatriate writing tends toward the spatial. The attempt, whether executed in Dos Passos' self-conscious cubism or Hemingway's, Stein's, Nin's, or Miller's less patently stylized yet innovative spatial forms, is to exhibit the variety and richness of a place so far as the place exists as a condition of thought, emotion, and memory. This requires adopting a form that substitutes for the temporal and causal emphasis of most narrative an emphasis on the fragmented and discontinuous parts of the Paris moment that make up its meaning as a whole. In some of the most striking expatriate spatial forms, such as those of Hemingway's and Stein's memoirs, Nin's *Diary,* and Miller's *Tropic of Cancer,* the representation of the discovery of a place is made equal in time and meaning with the discovery of a personal aesthetic, of a way of expressing oneself, with the product of this union the spatial work we are reading. It is this engaging and significant interplay between artist, place, and innovative self-reflexive forms that constitutes the most distinctive contribution of expatriate writing to the literary movement we have come to call high modernism.

SELECTED BIBLIOGRAPHY

Primary Works

Included here are major memoirs and novels by authors not examined in this study. For a much more inclusive list of expatriate writing, see William G. Bailey, *Americans in Paris, 1900–1930: A Selected Annotated Bibliography* (New York, 1989).

Bald, Wambly. *On the Left Bank, 1929–1933*. Athens, Ohio, 1987.

Barnes, Djuna. *Nightwood*. 1937; rpr. New York, 1946.

Beach, Sylvia. *Shakespeare and Company*. New York, 1959.

Braque, Georges, *et al.* "Testimony Against Gertrude Stein." *Transition*, XXIII (July, 1935), Supplement.

Callaghan, Morley. *That Summer in Paris*. New York, 1963.

Cowley, Malcolm. *Exile's Return: A Narrative of Ideas*. New York, 1934.

Crosby, Caresse. *The Passionate Years*. 1953; rpr. New York, 1979.

Cummings, E. E. *i—six nonlectures*. Cambridge, Mass., 1953.

Dos Passos, John. *The Best Times: An Informal Memoir*. New York, 1966.

Fitzgerald, Zelda. *Save Me the Waltz*. 1932; rpr. Carbondale, Ill., 1967.

Flanner, Janet. *Paris Was Yesterday, 1925–1939*. New York, 1972.

Josephson, Matthew. *Life Among the Surrealists*. New York, 1962.

Loeb, Harold. *The Way It Was*. New York, 1959.

McAlmon, Robert, and Kate Boyle. *Being Geniuses Together, 1920–1930*. 1968; rpr. San Francisco, 1984.

Miller, Linda P., ed. *Letters from the Lost Generation: Gerald and Sara Murphy and Friends*. New Brunswick, N.J., 1991.

Munson, Gorham. *The Awakening Twenties: A Memoir-History of a Literary Period*. Baton Rouge, 1985.

Stearns, Harold. *The Street I Know*. New York, 1935.

Toklas, Alice B. *What Is Remembered*. New York, 1963.

Secondary Works

Included here are general accounts of the expatriate movement. Works about the particular writers examined in this study are listed in the footnotes.

Bailey, William G. *Americans in Paris, 1900–1930: A Selected Annotated Bibliography.* New York, 1989.

Benstock, Shari. *Women of the Left Bank: Paris, 1900–1940.* Austin, Tex., 1986.

Bradbury, Malcolm. *The Expatriate Tradition in American Literature.* Durham, Eng., 1982.

Carpenter, Humphrey. *Geniuses Together: American Writers in Paris in the 1920s.* London, 1987.

Fabre, Michel. *From Harlem to Paris: Black American Writers in France, 1840–1980.* Urbana, Ill., 1991.

Fitch, Noël Riley. *Sylvia Beach and the Lost Generation: A History of Literary Paris in the Twenties and Thirties.* New York, 1983.

Ford, Hugh D. *Published in Paris: American and British Writers, Printers, and Publishers in Paris, 1920–1939.* New York, 1975.

Hansen, Arlen J. *Expatriate Paris: A Cultural and Literary Guide to Paris of the 1920s.* New York, 1990.

Kennedy, J. Gerald. *Imagining Paris: Exile, Writing, and American Identity.* New Haven, 1993.

McMahon, Joseph H. "City for Expatriates." *Yale French Studies,* XXXII (1964), 144–58.

Méral, Jean. *Paris in American Literature.* Chapel Hill, N.C., 1989.

Morton, Brian N. *Americans in Paris.* New York, 1986.

Rood, Karen, ed. *American Writers in Paris, 1920–1939.* Detroit, 1980. Vol. IV of *Dictionary of Literary Biography.*

Tucker, Martin. *Literary Exile in the Twentieth Century: An Analysis and Biographical Dictionary.* New York, 1991.

Wickes, George. *Americans in Paris.* Garden City, N.Y., 1969.

INDEX

Allendy, René, 51–53, 62–64, 66, 69, 70, 71
Anderson, Sherwood, 46
Androgyny, 53, 57–62, 66
Apollinaire, Guillaume, 36, 47
Artaud, Antonin, 51–53, 64–65, 71
—"The Theatre and the Plague," 64

Bald, Wambly, 133*n*7
Barnes, Djuna, xiv, 80
—*Nightwood,* xiv
Barney, Natalie, 11, 24, 25, 80, 114*n*8
Beach, Sylvia, 16, 21–22, 24, 46
Benstock, Shari, xiii*n*1
Bergson, Henri, 34
Bourne, Randolph, 92
Boyle, Kate, xiv
—*Being Geniuses Together,* xiv
Bradley, William, 51
Braque, Georges, 35
Bromfield, Louis, 47
Brooks, Romaine, 114*n*8

Cézanne, Paul, 11, 16, 35, 38, 39, 42, 43
Columbia University, 92
Copeland, Charles T. (Copey), 92, 93
Cowley, Malcolm, xiv
—*Exile's Return,* xiv

Defoe, Daniel, 27
—*Robinson Crusoe,* 27

Dos Passos, John, xiv, 3, 18, 24, 46, 73–76, 86–103, 141–43
—*The Big Money,* 87, 103; *The 42nd Parallel,* 87; *Nineteen-Nineteen,* 73–76, 86–103, 142; *Three Soldiers,* 3, 90–91; *U.S.A.,* 87
Dunning, Cheever, 22, 26

Eliot, T. S., 24, 46, 47, 76
Emerson, Ralph Waldo, 136
Expatriate writing: American values in, 1–6, 14, 16, 21, 32, 63, 102–103, 104–105, 113, 132, 142; autobiography and fiction in, compared, xv, 73–76, 91, 123–24, 136, 142; cubist and spatial forms in, xiv, 8–9, 25, 34–36, 38, 40, 44, 89, 91, 125–26, 142–43; and drama of consciousness, xiv, 32–34, 70, 87, 142; hunger and sustenance trope in, 14–19, 43, 79, 123, 130–31, 142; mobility trope in, 10–11, 51, 55–57, 77–78, 80, 81, 86, 123, 128, 135–39, 142; and personal aesthetic, 16, 40, 53, 66–67, 72, 126–27, 133, 136, 139, 143; sexuality and creative potency in, xiv, 11–14, 31, 60–62, 73, 80–81, 85–86, 93–94, 97, 99–101, 113, 116–19, 132–34, 142

Faÿ, Bernard, 48
Fernande. *See* Olivier, Fernande